GW00684745

Adobe Experience Manager

web content management

[Formerly CQ]

QUICK-REFERENCE GUIDE

Shane Closser

ADOBE PRESS

Adobe

ADOBE® EXPERIENCE MANAGER QUICK-REFERENCE GUIDE
Web Content Management (formerly CQ)
Shane Closser

Adobe Press books are published by Peachpit, a division of Pearson Education.

For the latest on Adobe Press books, go to www.adobepress.com.

To report errors, please send a note to errata@peachpit.com.

Copyright © 2014 by Adobe Press

Adobe Press Editor: Victor Gavenda
Project Editor: Clifford Colby
Development Editor: Stacey Closser
Copyeditor: Darren Meiss
Production Editor: Katerina Malone
Compositor: David Van Ness
Indexer: Valerie Haynes Perry
Cover and Interior design: Mimi Heft
Additional contributions: Nikhil Gupta, Yogesh Mulwani, Manivannan Karunanithi, Prithwiraj Deb, Palkesh Khandelwal, and Maria Sylvia Petzold

Printed and bound in the United States of America

ISBN 13: 978-0-321-96781-7
ISBN 10:   0-321-96781-X

9 8 7 6 5 4 3 2 1

To Mom and Joe, who remain guiding lights in my life;
to my editor and wife Stacey, who encouraged me to write;
and to my children Jack and Avery, who fill my days
with laughter and joy.

About the Author

 Shane Closser is Vice President & Worldwide Head for the Customer Experience Management (CEM) Practice at Virtusa Corp (NASDAQ:VRTU), a global IT services company that combines innovation, technology leadership and industry solutions to transform the customer experience. He manages over 500 CEM experts worldwide, who develop advanced solutions for Virtusa's media, financial services, insurance and healthcare customers. Closser has managed over 75 programs across Fortune 500 organizations. He is a frequent speaker on CEM strategy, digital marketing, mobile, social and WCM. He is an Adobe-certified trainer, and he has over 15 years of experience leading digital engagements. Connect with him on Linkedin or via Twitter @srclosser.

Contents at a Glance

Contents

1
Why Adobe Experience Manager (AEM)?

Over the last few years, we have seen websites evolve from static brochureware sites to dynamically changing digital marketing suites that are competing in an arena where the competition is a click away. In a short amount of time, some of the biggest brands across industries have evaporated into Chapter 11 because they refused to risk their brick and mortar cash cows by moving their businesses online.

To meet the challenges of today and needs of tomorrow, businesses have to be agile, adaptable, and innovative. They are turning to technologies like Adobe Experience Manager (AEM) to remain competitive.

AEM allows organizations to create a compelling online experience across digital channels—web, mobile, email, video, web analytics, and social media. This digital marketing suite helps organizations build their brand, drive revenue, and extend their reach.

Adobe Experience Manager empowers organizations to:

- Build brand: Target and personalize messages, offers, and your online user experience while maintaining brand consistency.

- Drive revenue: Listen to your users' social expressions and sentiments, and monitor user behavior in order to create meaningful campaigns for different user segments or demographics to drive conversions.

- Extend reach: Interact and reach customers across web, mobile, and social channels.

Adobe AEM Core Features

Adobe Experience Manager (AEM) is the Adobe Marketing Cloud solution for building digital properties across web, mobile, social, email, and video channels. AEM was formerly known as Adobe CQ. AEM offers web content management, digital asset management, social communities, and mobile capabilities.

Web Content Management

Adobe offers a user-friendly application so marketers can easily author, manage, and deliver content to online channels. This removes the historical dependency on IT to publish content, images, and videos online. It provides a single hub for all your online content that can be reused across websites or digital channels.

This is the welcome screen for Adobe AEM where you can access all major interfaces for the product. You will be redirected here after you log in. The left navigation will contain the main links for business users including websites, digital assets, tagging, and campaigns. The right side is mostly administrative and developer links.

Clicking the Websites link on the welcome screen opens this console, which allows you to access all websites, webpages, digital assets, and campaigns. On the left is a list of websites; click a plus sign to explore the webpages within these websites.

Digital Asset Management

The AEM digital asset management (DAM) solution provides an intuitive interface to upload, manipulate, manage, and tag digital assets with relevant information. Features include a framework that automates common required actions, such as resizing images.

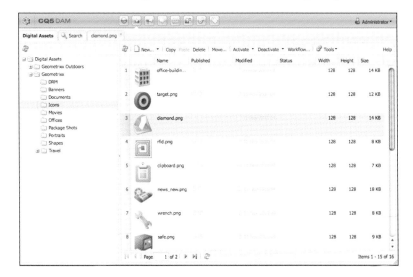

In the main page for the AEM DAM, you can manage all digital assets, which include images, videos, and so on. Use the folder structure to navigate the classification systems used to manage digital assets.

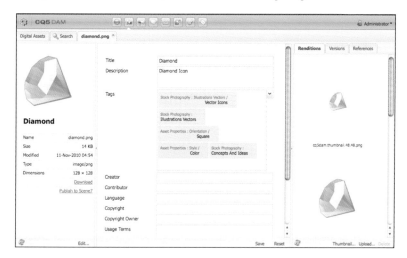

Once you select a digital asset, you'll be able to manage its properties, such as titles, descriptions, and tags.

Social and Communities

AEM offers social tools needed to engage users around your company's products, services, and content. It does this with features like blogs, shared calendars, ratings, reviews, and social login. Social login is the ability to use your Facebook or Twitter logins to authenticate against AEM managed web properties.

Social is an emerging area in Adobe AEM. The social component shown here allows for user-generated content and can be completely customized to your website needs and brand.

Mobile Delivery

You will see Adobe's products from AEM 5.6 onward focus on a mobile-first strategy. Within AEM 5.5 you can manage how your content is presented to the thousands of different mobile devices on the market.

Adobe AEM provides a rich user interface to manage your mobile channel. This is the content author screen for mobile devices. Simply click a mobile device (such as a smart phone, feature phone, or tablet) to see how your website's content is rendered on it.

What Is the Adobe Marketing Cloud?

Adobe has created a suite of products for digital marketers. The Adobe Marketing Cloud is comprised of five product lines, which include analytics, social, advertising, targeting, and web experience management. These products can be purchased and used separately or as an integrated bundle. Together they create a seamless online experience that listens for customer insights, predicts what they will want, assembles this content (such as rates, offers, and campaigns), and delivers it to the appropriate digital channel (web, mobile, social, email, and so on).

For more information on the Adobe Marketing Cloud please refer to www.adobe.com/marketingcloud.

This is the Adobe Marketing Cloud and its five core solutions:

• Adobe Social: Allows marketing teams to measure and manage social content across paid, earned, and owned media and channels.

• Adobe Analytics: Gives you empirical data to benchmark and track your success across channels. Now you can answer those management questions around how effective your web presence is at building awareness, acquiring business, driving engagement, and ultimately selling products and services online.

• Adobe Target: Success is about delivering the right content, to the right person, at the right time. Adobe Target allows you to test what works and personalize this content to different user segments.

• Adobe Experience Manager: What this book is all about

• Adobe Media Optimizer: Empowers organizations to build rules to optimize ad management, set targets against marketing forecasts, and optimize marketing campaigns to drive revenue.

Useful Resources

When you run into issues or have questions, use these resources for documentation or support:

- Technical documents:

  http://dev.day.com/docs

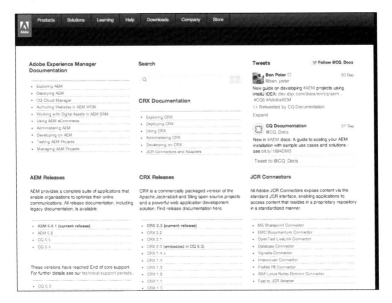

Make sure to bookmark this webpage; you will access it frequently as you open tickets on the platform, learn more about the product, or seek answers to common questions.

- Knowledge Base:

  http://dev.day.com/kb

- Support:

  http://daycare.day.com (login required)

2

AEM Key Concepts

This chapter highlights the core content management concepts within Adobe Experience Manager (AEM), including installing AEM, exploring the content management interfaces, discussing how to create and manage content, outlining common roles, publishing content, and discussing content inheritance. This information will provide the foundation to study more advanced AEM topics.

Installing Adobe AEM

Install AEM on your machine so you have a safe haven to play with the software, which is the best way to master the product. You can get the software through your Adobe sales representative, your IT team, or through the Adobe website (https://licensing.adobe.com).

Installation prerequisites:

- CQ5 quickstart JAR
- Valid CQ5 license
- JDK 1.6 or higher
- Approximately 800 MB of free disk space
- Approximately 1 GB of RAM (preferably more)

  TIP ▶ For more-detailed information on technical requirements, see http://dev.day.com/.

To install AEM:

1 Create a folder structure for your Authoring instance. Do not use spaces in your newly created folder structure on Windows, as it will create an error. For example, you can use the folder structure C:/AEM56/author.

2 Copy your Adobe AEM JAR and license.properties files into this newly created folder structure.

Mac folder structure

3 Rename the AEM quickstart JAR to *aem561-author-4502.jar,*
where *aem* is the application, and *author* is the WCM mode it will
run in (for example, author or publish). 4502 is the port to run
AEM in (although any available port is acceptable).

4 Double-click the aem561-author-4502.jar file. The installation
will take a few minutes.

When the installation is done, the Adobe AEM login screen
pops up.

5 Repeat these steps to install the publish instance, but remember
to make these few changes:

• Create a folder structure for your publish instance C:/
AEM56/publish.

• Copy your jar and license file into this publish folder.

• Rename the JAR file to *aem-publish-4503.jar.* Notice the use of
publish instead of author for WCM mode, and different port
number.

6 Double-click the aem-publish-4503.jar file to finish the
installation.

TIP ► You can also start Adobe AEM from the command line by
entering java -Xmx512m -jar aem561-author-4502.jar.

7 Begin by logging into AEM.

TIP ▶ When the login page opens, bookmark the page since you will use it daily. If you have installed a local version of AEM, the default URL will be http://localhost:4502/ for the Author instance. The default username and password is admin/admin.

Author and Publish instance

It's important to understand the difference between an Author and Publish instance, as both of them will be referenced throughout this book.

Author instance

The Author instance is an internal instance of Adobe AEM that allows your organization's internal teams to create, edit, delete, move, and manage content. Content authors can make changes to this internal copy of your website and preview without having these changes visible on your public website. When this content has been internally approved, it can be published to the production environment.

Publish instance

The Publish instance allows content to be viewed publicly after it's been approved through an organization's content creation process. Visitors can interact with the website and consume information, post comments, and access with digital assets.

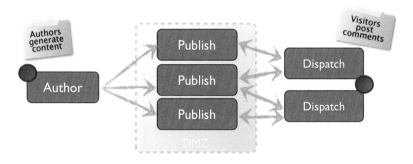

This book will almost exclusively focus on managing content for business users, so this is the closest you will get to seeing a logical architecture diagram. *(Image Courtesy of Adobe)*

User interfaces

There are over 5,000 different mobile devices, with several more devices being added to the market every week. Adobe realizes that more and more of their customers—busy knowledge workers on the move—prefer to manage content on mobile devices. This trend is only expected to grow, so starting with AEM 5.6, Adobe has adopted a mobile-first strategy.

Adobe is modernizing the AEM interface to support mobile through its touch-optimized user interface (UI). All content management features are not supported in AEM 5.6 touch-optimized UI. As new AEM product versions are released, the touch-optimized UI will be expanded to support all content management features. Until then you will still need to use the classic UI view or desktop version.

Touch-optimized UI

You will know you are in touch-optimized UI if you have a black-and-gray background. Content is arranged in a card view. With a touch-enabled device, you can navigate through the interface with the following actions: tap, tap and hold, and swipe.

Search: Enter a keyword search for content items.

Switch to Classic view: Switch from touch-optimized to classic view.

Console Timeline: Recently edited items

Select Mode: Enter and Exit icons for Select Mode feature. Use it to manage individual content items.

Notifications: The number indicates number of notifications.

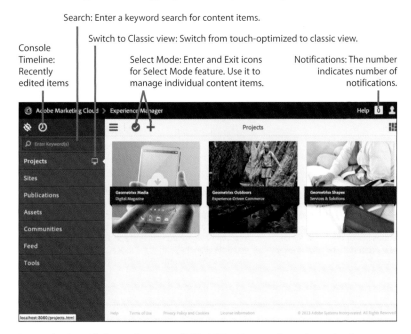

Page authoring with the touch-optimized UI in AEM 5.6 is currently preview technology. It should not be used for production instances. There are subtle differences between the 5.6 and 5.6.1 user interfaces, but the concepts taught in this book will apply to both.

Table 2.1 Touch-Optimized UI Main Screens

LINK	DESCRIPTION
Projects/Welcome Screen	Projects are used to group resources such as sites, assets, mobile sites, and communities together.
Sites	Allows you to navigate through websites, and create and manage pages
Publications	Accesses Media Publisher, an AEM add-on designed for creating and managing media and publishing content
Assets	Allows you to navigate and manage your digital assets
Collections	This link becomes available after you select the Asset console. It's used to manage collections of assets.
Communities	Allows you to manage and moderate community forums
Feed	Links to the Adobe Marketing Cloud Feed console
Tools	Accesses the various tools available to manage content

Quick actions: Either hover over with the mouse pointer or tap and hold to review quick actions like open in edit mode, view properties, or copy, move, or publish pages.

Breadcrumb: As you enter into a site, you can navigate up multiple branches using the breadcrumb.

Card or List view: View all pages in a Card view, which is displayed here. You can also switch to the List view to display an infinite list, which is easier for viewing large data sets of information.

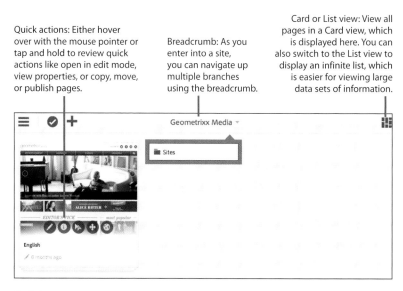

Card view

How to change the default UI mode

If you want to change the default UI mode you can do this one of two ways. The first method is to set your UI preferences in User Preferences:

1   Click the person icon, and then click Account.

2   Choose your preferred Authoring Mode and click Save.

In the second method, your administrator sets UI preferences. The Classic UI is the preferred model for production environments. You can use this method to set production UI preferences for all users:

1   Have your administrator update the DAY CQ Root Mapping within the OSGI configuration screen. Change Target Path to /projects.html for touch-optimized UI or /welcome.html for the classic UI.

2   You can switch to classic UI view by selecting the desktop icon in the right Rail. It will appear only when you hover or tap and hold the menu item.

Classic UI

The classic UI, or desktop version, is distinguished by a green header and provides all content management features in a classic link-based system.

The Websites console, accessible via the link at the top of the list, is where AEM users spend most of their time managing their webpages.

Websites console

The Websites console is the main content author screen to manage websites. Icons at the top of the console provide quick links to all the other AEM features listed on the home page.

Digital Assets or DAM console: The digital asset management system is where all digital assets are store and managed. Chapter 4 covers this feature.

Communities: Manage user-generated content (UGC) such as ratings and reviews.

Campaigns: Manage marketing campaigns that AEM can display through personalization efforts.

Inbox: Interface for managing tasks assigned to content authors and editors

Users: Manage users, groups, and permissions

Search: Granular search controls to find content based on permissions

Tools: AEM configuration tools such as reports, managing packages, workflows, and so on.

Tags: Location to manage all tags and taxonomies for AEM

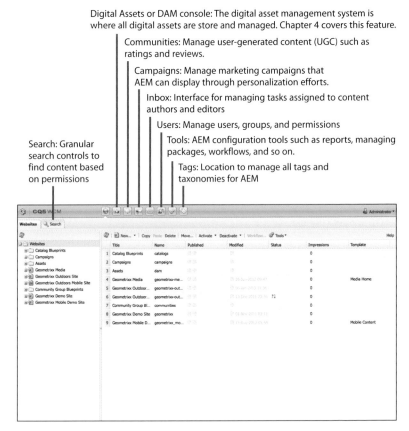

Website interface. If any of the icons are grayed out, it means you don't have permission to these features.

WEBSITE HIERARCHY

Navigate and manage websites and their structural relationships from the left side of the Websites console. You can expand or collapse the different content nodes to drill into the structure and view pages.

PAGE INFORMATION

The Website console provides the ability to manage pages. Double-click a page to open in edit mode or right-click the page name and select Open.

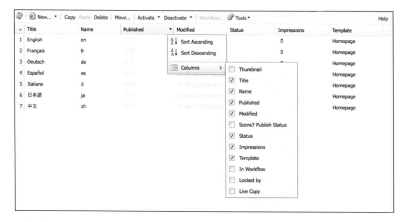

By clicking the Columns tab, you can select which properties are displayed in the resulting list or order the columns based on your preference.

3
Managing Content

Every website is comprised of thousands of pieces of content, which are personalized, assembled, and delivered into webpages. These webpages form the digital experience visitors interact with online.

In this chapter, you will learn how to create and manage pages. The chapter explores the AEM tools that enable content contributors to perform their job duties.

Creating content

Creating content is what Adobe Experience Manager was designed for. Its tools, features, and capabilities help to create websites that are cross-channel and personalized to different audiences.

NOTE ▶ Both the touch UI and classic UI can be used to perform many of these functions. Throughout this book, you'll mostly see examples with the classic UI since the touch UI is still considered a preview technology. This means it's not fully supported, nor should it be enabled in production.

How to create a website

1   From the AEM home page, click Websites (or click the Websites icon on the AEM toolbar).

2   On the toolbar, click the New button and choose New Site.

Websites console

3 Create a site title and name. Select the site blueprint and click Next.

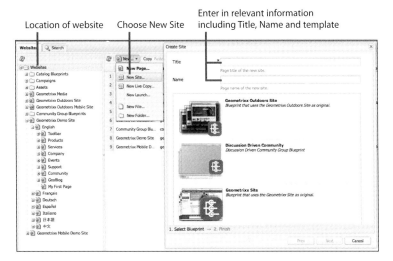

Create a new website

4 Select appropriate languages of the blueprint. Select the chapters of the blueprint you want to copy to a new site. Select the site owner.

5 Select whether you want the site to be a live copy. Optionally, you can select rollout configs. Refer to Chapter 7 for more information on these options.

6 Click Create Site. A new website has been created and will show up in the websites list on the left.

How to create a webpage

1 From the AEM home page, click Websites to open the Websites interface.

This is where your websites and webpages are displayed a hierarchical tree in the left pane.

Websites tree list on left side of Websites interface

NOTE ▶ The Websites tree list is used to navigate websites and pages. You can click the plus sign or minus sign to expand or close the list of pages in a website.

2 Click the New button and choose New Page.

New Page link—If you do not see this option, make sure you've selected a website you have permission to create pages in.

3 In the Create Page dialog box, enter the desired Title and Name for the new page and select the appropriate template.

Create Page dialog box—The Title is displayed to users and the Name is used to generate the URI (which is part of the URL).

4 Confirm that the new page was created in the correct place by navigating back through the website tree hierarchy to find your page. Double-click the page to open it in edit mode.

How to edit a page

1   From the AEM home page, click Websites (or click the Websites icon on the AEM toolbar). Double-click the page you'd like to edit, or right-click the name and choose Open from the context menu.

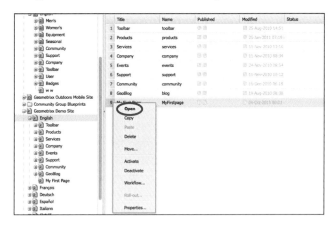

Open a page for edit

The page opens in edit mode. At this point, you have several ways to proceed.

Content Finder—Displays available images, manuscripts, documents, movies, products, pages, paragraphs, and Scene 7 media files.

Sidekick—Allows you to switch modes to manage different parts of a page.

Page title

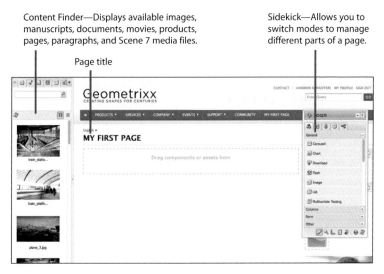

Edit mode

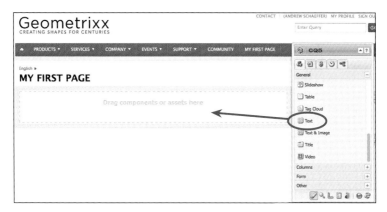

Add a component—When you try to drag a component onto a page, if it's not authorized to be in the section, you will see a red circle with a line through it.

As you hover the pointer over parts of a page, the region turns green, which means you can edit this section. There are three ways to edit a section:

- Double-click the section to open a window with available components you can add.

- Right-click the section and choose New from the context menu, which brings up the component window.

- Use the Sidekick. Find the component you want to add and drop it in the correct section. In this example, the Text component is added.

Type in text and click OK.

Text component

2 After dropping the desired component onto the page, to manage the content double-click it, or right-click and choose Edit from the context menu.

In this example, a text editor was added that allows for text entry on the page.

3 Make your changes and click OK.

How to use Content Finder

Content Finder allows you to you to find images, manuscripts, documents, movies, products, pages, paragraphs, and Scene 7 Media files.

Search—Use the Content Finder to search for different types of files. You can use the search field to find files. In this example, the word *train* was used as the search term.

Search results

Drag and drop desired asset onto the page.

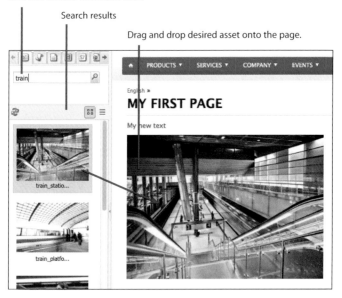

Content Finder

NOTE ▶ If you see a red circle with a line through it when you attempt to drag and drop images or other files onto a page, you don't have permission to place that asset in that area of the page.

How to use the Sidekick

The Sidekick will be your best friend and remote control for managing and editing pages. You can use it to switch the page modes (from edit to preview, for example), edit metadata about the page, and construct parts of the page. Feel free to move it around or minimize it if it gets in your way.

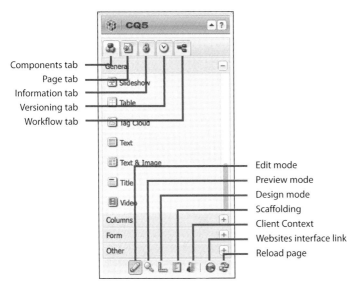

Components tab
Page tab
Information tab
Versioning tab
Workflow tab

Edit mode
Preview mode
Design mode
Scaffolding
Client Context
Websites interface link
Reload page

Sidekick—If you don't see an AEM component you know is available, you probably need to go into design mode and activate the component.

TIP ▶ At times your Sidekick may start to act irrational and not work right. When this happens try refreshing the page, and if that doesn't work clear your cookies and restart your browser.

COMPONENTS TAB

View the available components to add on the page. An accordion menu includes categories for components. Remember, if you're allowed to drag and drop a component into a region, you'll see a green border around the region. If you see a red circle with a line through it, the component is not allowed in that region or paragraph system.

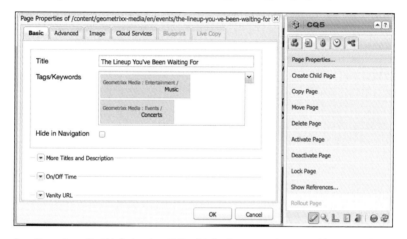

Page Properties—Use this feature to edit the details of a page such as page title, tags, and page description. If it's a mobile template, you'll also see a Mobile tab.

PAGE TAB

This is where you control page settings. You can also activate a page, which moves it from author to publish or your public website. It also allows you to edit Page Properties.

INFORMATION TAB

From here, you can view the audit history and manage permissions associated with the page, such as who can read, update, delete, and create content.

VERSIONING TAB

This tab allows you to view your version history, create versions, restore versions, and view content differences between versions. Launches allow you to create a copy of a website, branch of a website, or a page you want to work on simultaneously. Timewarp allows you to view back in time to see what the page looked like on a specific date.

Versioning tab

WORKFLOW TAB

Initiate a workflow or start a workflow translation.

EDIT MODE

Makes it possible to edit content on a page.

PREVIEW MODE

When you are in edit mode, the UI is not pixel perfect. But by entering preview mode, you can view the page as a visitor would see it. If the page is using responsive design, you can also select different device types to see how the page conforms to different widths.

DESIGN MODE

In this mode, you can control what components are authorized for a page.

Edit the logo displayed on all pages.

Edit top-level navigation, or what level of the website to base the navigation on.

Activate components that are allowed to be used for a region within the page. For example, if you select the Carousel checkbox, it will appear in the Sidekick.

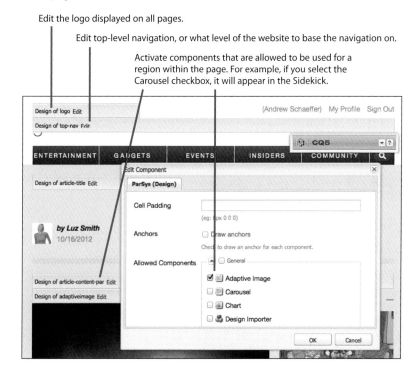

Design mode allows you to control design elements of the page.

SCAFFOLDING

When you need to edit a large set of pages that have the same structure, using the scaffolding interface is often easier. Scaffolding allows you to edit the content on the page in form layout versus editing it in context where you need to double-click each component, enter text, and then click Save.

CLIENT CONTEXT

Control the personalization elements of a webpage with Client Context. You can emulate actions on a website to see how the page transforms its appearance. For example, how would a page be personalized if a user logged in to the page?

Client Context

Managing page structure

Now that you've begun to create your website, you may find the need to relocate pages or assets. The flexibility afforded by AEM makes this an easy task.

How to move a page

1 Open the Websites interface and select the page that needs to be moved. Click the Move button in the AEM toolbar, or right-click the page and choose Move from the context menu.

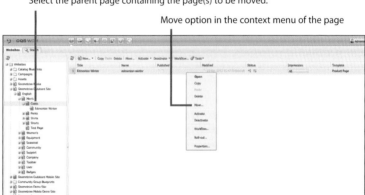

Select the parent page containing the page(s) to be moved.

Move option in the context menu of the page

Move a page

2 In the Move dialog box, click the search icon in the To field to select a target location where the page should be moved.

3 In the Select Path dialog box, Click OK.

Note that AEM automatically adjusts all the associated paths references of this page wherever it is being used.

4   Click Move to move the page to desired location.

OK button sets the
desired path of the move.

Move button finalizes the changes.

References of page to be moved   Select target path.

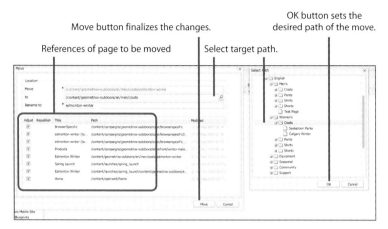

Move a page

TIP ▶   You can simply move a page by dragging and dropping the
page to a desired folder or parent page.

How to reorder a page

1   In the Websites interface, select the page that needs to be reordered and simply drag it to the desired location in the page
hierarchy.

System notifies that selected page is getting reordered

The system shows a prompt to confirm the action.

2 Click Yes to confirm the changes.

Yes/No dialog box to confirm or cancel the changes

How to copy and paste a page

1 From the Websites interface, select the page that needs to be copied and click the Copy button in the AEM toolbar, or right-click the page and choose Copy from the context menu.

Select the parent page containing the page(s) to be copied.

Copy button on AEM toolbar

Copy option in the context menu of the page

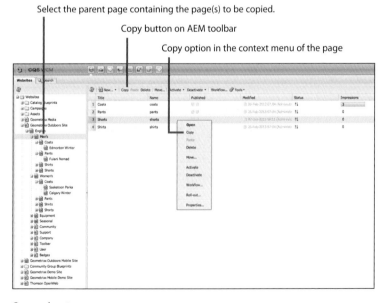

Copy and paste a page

2 After the page has been copied, the Paste button is enabled on the AEM toolbar. Navigate to a desired folder path and click the Paste button to replicate the copied page in the new location.

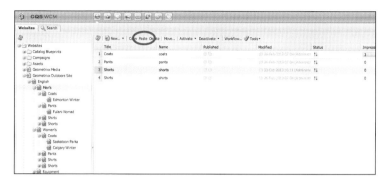

Paste button is enabled in the toolbar.

How to delete a page

1 From the Websites interface, select the page that needs to be deleted and click the Delete button in the AEM toolbar, or right-click menu the page and choose Delete from the context menu.

Select the parent page containing the page(s) to be deleted.

Delete button on AEM toolbar

Delete option in the context menu

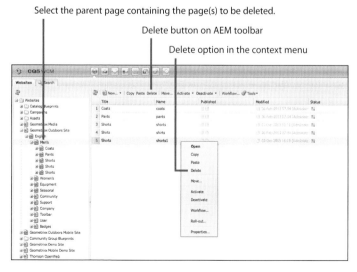

Delete page

2 Click Yes to confirm the page deletion.

Confirm or cancel the deletion.

3 If the page to be deleted has references, the system will prompt you to review these references or continue deleting the page.

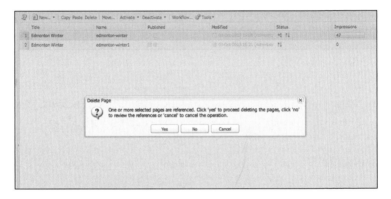

Click Yes to proceed deleting page or click No to review page references.

How to search for pages

There are a couple ways you can search for pages, which are highlighted in the following sections.

SEARCH BY FULLTEXT

To search for pages by Fulltext, click the Search tab in the AEM window. Type the name of the page you want to search for and press Enter.

Search tab in AEM window

Text box to enter the page name to be searched

Search results

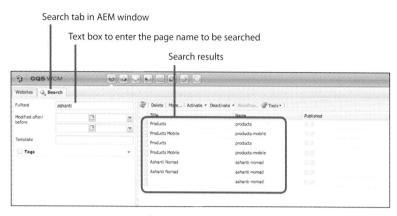

Search by Fulltext

SEARCH BY TAGS

Searching by tags allows user to search for pages that have a defined metadata tag associated with them. Click the Tags drop-down to see a list of available tags in the system and select the desired tags for which pages needs to be searched against.

In this example, swimming is the search tag. The system displays all the pages that have Swimming as a defined tag.

Tag to search by   Search results

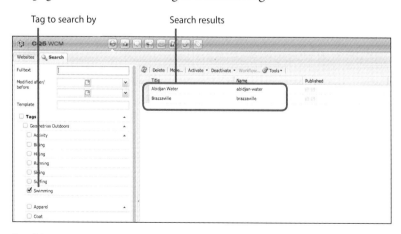

Search by tags

SEARCH BY MODIFIED AFTER/BEFORE AND DATE/TIME

You can also search for relevant pages based on when they were modified. Select a date and time range in the Modified After/Before fields and press Enter.

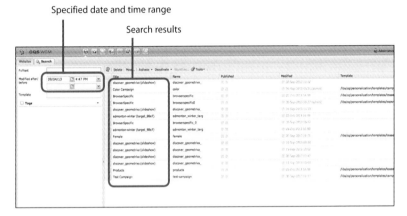

Search by modification details

How to lock a page

AEM allows you to lock down a page for editing by other users.

1 From the Websites interface, select the page you want to lock. Right-click the page and choose Open from the context menu (or double-click the page) to open it.

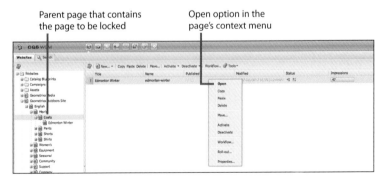

Web page to be locked down

2 On the Sidekick, click the Page tab and select Lock Page to lock the page for editing by other users.

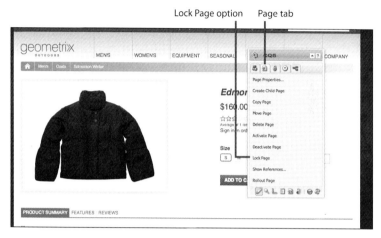

Lock page option in Sidekick

3 Hover the mouse pointer on the page's Status column to see that the page is locked.

Locked page

How to unlock a page

1   From the Websites interface, select the page you want to unlock. Right-click the page and choose Open from the context menu (or double-click the page) to open it.

2   On the Sidekick, click the Page tab and select Unlock Page to unlock the page for editing by other users.

    TIP ▶ You can only unlock locked pages if you were the one who locked them or if you have administrator privileges.

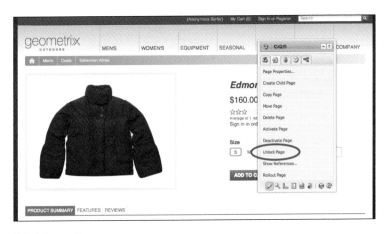

Unlock Page option

How to activate a page

1   From the Websites interface, select the page you want to activate and click the Activate button in the AEM toolbar, or right-click the page and choose Activate from the context menu.

    NOTE ▶ When you activate a page it is published to the website, so it can be viewed by site visitors.

Select the parent page that contains
the page(s) you want to activate

Activate option in the AEM toolbar
and context menu

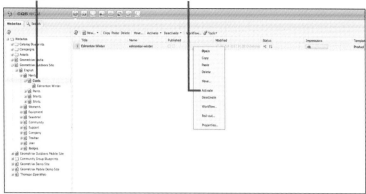

Activate a page

2 AEM notifies you to activate any associated images, campaigns, and configurations as well. Click Activate.

Activate button to activate the selected page and associated assets

The system marks the page for activation and moves it in the activation queue for the publish instance.

Page in the activation queue

TIP ▶ A user can also activate a page directly from Sidekick. Navigate to the Page tab and select Activate Page.

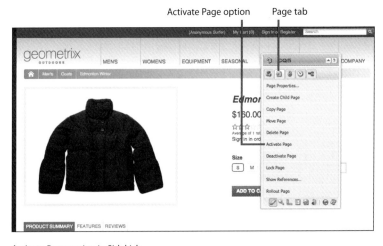

Activate Page option in Sidekick

How to schedule a page for activation

AEM provides functionality to set a schedule for page activation at a later time/future date.

1　From the Websites interface, select the page that needs to be activated. Click the Activate button in the AEM toolbar and choose Activate Later from the drop-down menu.

Select the parent page containing the page(s) you want to activate later.

Selected page　Activate button with drop-down

Activate Later option

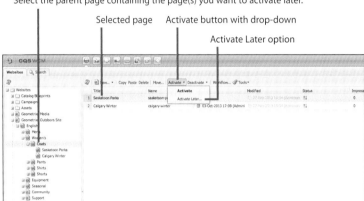

Activate Later option

2　In the Activate Later dialog box, select a desired activation date and time and click OK.

Activation　OK button sets the
date and time　activation date/time

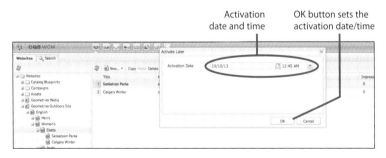

Activate Later dialog box

AEM notifies you that the page has been marked for activation on a later date on mouse-over for that particular page.

System notifying you on mouse-over that the page is marked for activation for a later date

How to deactivate a page

1   From the Websites interface, select the page you want to deactivate. Right-click the page and choose Deactivate from the context menu, or click the Deactivate button in the AEM toolbar

     NOTE ▶ Deactivating a page removes it from the public website, so it will not be viewable by site visitors.

Select the parent page containing the page(s) you want to deactivate

Deactivate option in the AEM toolbar and context menu of the page

Deactivating a page

2 Click Yes to confirm the page deactivation.

Confirm page deactivation

AEM notifies users that the page has been marked for deactivation upon doing a mouse-over on the Status column for that particular page.

System notifying the page is in deactivation queue

TIP ► A user can also deactivate a page directly from Sidekick. Open the page in edit mode and click the Page tab. Select Deactivate Page.

Deactivate Page option   Page tab

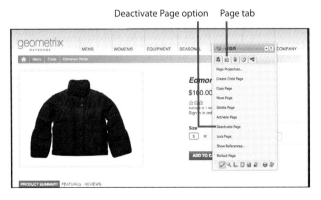

Deactivate Page via the Sidekick

How to schedule a page for deactivation

AEM provides functionality to set a schedule for page deactivation for deactivation on a later/future date.

1 From the Websites interface, select the page you want to deactivate. Click the Deactivate button in the AEM toolbar and choose Deactivate Later from the drop-down menu.

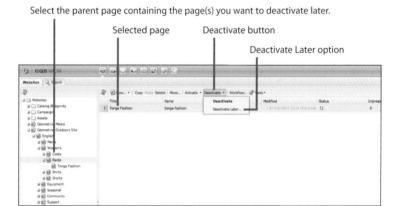

Deactivate Later option

2 In the Deactivate Later dialog box, select a desired deactivation date and time and click OK.

Deactivate Later dialog box

AEM notifies users that the page has been marked for deactivation on a later date upon doing a mouse-over on the Status column for that particular page.

System notifying page is marked for deactivation for a later date

How to activate a complete section of your website

When you want to activate several pages at a time, you can do so in the Tools interface.

1 Go into Tools interface from the home page or from the top navigation of the Websites console.

2 Click Replication to expand the tree.

3 Double-click the Activate Tree page. Select the content you want to publish. If you expand the content folder, you will see all websites available for publish. Click the Activate button.

Activate Tree tool

NOTE ▶ You can click the Dry Run option to emulate an activation; it will show you which pages will be activated.

Versioning

Versioning allows you to save copies of pages. Often people create copies of pages when they publish them or when they've made a major update. This allows you to refer back to these versions at a later time or even compare different versions against each other.

How to create a version

1   From the Websites interface, select the page to be versioned from the page hierarchy. Double-click it to open it in edit mode, or right-click it and choose Open from the right-click menu.

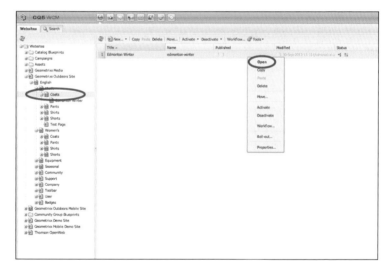

2 On the Sidekick, click the Versioning tab. After making relevant changes on the page, set the optional Label and Comment and click the Create Version button.

Create Version button   Versioning tab

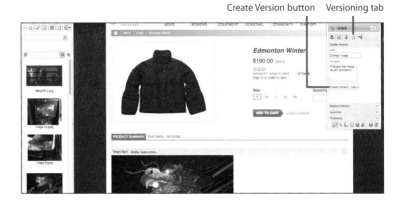

AEM notifies the user that the version has been created.

Version notification pop-up

How to restore a version

The Restore option is helpful when you want to revert the page back to a previous version.

1   To restore a version of the page you're working on, click the plus sign to expand the Restore Version area of the Versioning tab on Sidekick.

2   Select the desired version to restore and click the Restore button.

List of versions of the page   Restore button

3   Click Yes to confirm restoration of the page to the version selected.

Yes/No option in the Restore dialog box

How to compare versions

To preview and compare different versions of the same page, AEM provides functionality within the Restore Version area to preview a page before restoring it.

1 From the Versioning tab of the Sidekick, select the version you want to preview and click the Diff button to preview the page.

Comparing versions

AEM displays the page in preview mode. Note that all the versions are dimmed now until the user clicks the Back button to exit the preview mode.

Back button to exit the preview mode

Content launches

Launches are useful when you want to prepare multiple versions of a website at the same time and sync changes between them.

Consider the following use cases:

- You want to create a copy of the current content, so you can work on a big release for Thanksgiving.

- You want groups to be able to make any required changes to the existing website and activate them, without having your work impact them.

- You want to be able to edit the launch.

- You want content edited in the production version to sync with your launch version.

- When you are ready to promote your content, you can replace it in author and activate it when you're ready see it on your publish website.

How to manage a launch

1 In AEM, navigate to the following URL to create a launch: http://<<*server:portnumber*>>/libs/launches/content/admin.html

2 Click the New button to create a new launch.

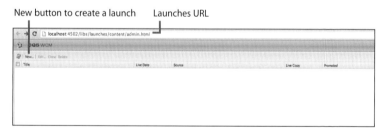

New button to create a launch   Launches URL

Launch Admin

3 Set the relevant launch title. In the Source Page field, click the search icon to set the page you want to launch.

4 Set the relevant launch date and time for the page to launch. Click Create to create the launch.

Launch date and time

Title for launch

Search icon to search for a launch page

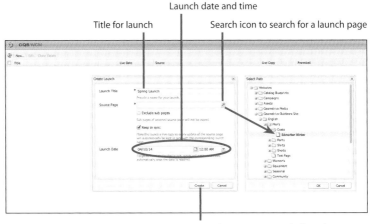

Launch Console

Create button to create the launch

NOTE ▶ Subpages will be included unless you select the Exclude Sub Pages option. Additionally, if you don't want to sync changes with production and your launch, deselect the Keep In Sync option.

5 Navigate back to the page for which launch was created and click the Versioning tab. Expand the Launches area.

Notice that the just-created launch is now visible in the available launches. User can switch to a different launch version and edit the content accordingly, which will be activated as per the desired dates set at time of launch creation.

Switch button to switch to
that launch to edit content

Select the desired launch

Timewarp

The Timewarp feature in AEM allows the user to see a history of page changes over a timeline and access to the previous versions.

How to use Timewarp

1   To see the Timewarp for a particular page, click the Versioning tab in AEM Sidekick and expand the Timewarp section.

2   Set a desired date and time and click the Show Timeline button to see a particular date's edits.

Show Timeline button displays a modal   Date and Time for which
showing a particular date's edits   Timewarp will be set

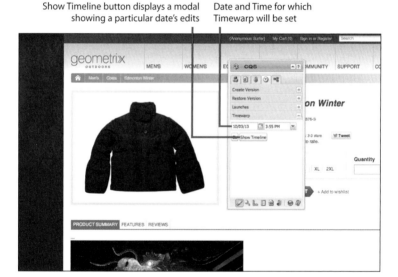

3 In the Timeline window, the user can see the changes performed on the page. Click the small blue icon to see the edit history (if available) for that page.

Timeline view with link to comments

4 Clicking the Go button displays the page that existed on that particular timestamp.

Comments on the page in a previous time   Go button to display the past page

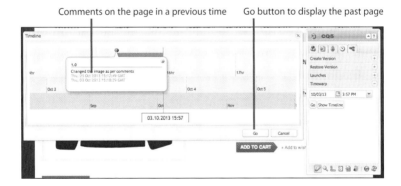

4
Digital Asset Management

Like other digital asset management systems (DAM), Adobe Experience Manager's DAM focuses on managing digital media files, but it excels in integrating these digital assets within Adobe's web content management system. The DAM is able to catalog and manage video files, images, or music files, each in their varying formats. When used properly, this feature will increase the overall value of AEM by simplifying integration of rich media into your web experience.

Basic DAM Functions

AEM provides powerful drag and drop functionality so you can upload images directly from a local machine or bulk upload multiple digital assets via Web DAV or Adobe Drive.

How to organize assets

The first step in organizing your assets is to create a logical folder structure:

1   On the AEM welcome screen, click the Digital Assets link.

Digital Asset Management link

2   In the AEM DAM folder structure, select the site where you want to upload or manage the assets.

3   In the toolbar, click New, and choose New Folder to create a new folder with a relevant name, such as video, document, image, and so on.

AEM folder structure   New Folder menu item under
for a site in the DAM   the New button on toolbar   Folder created

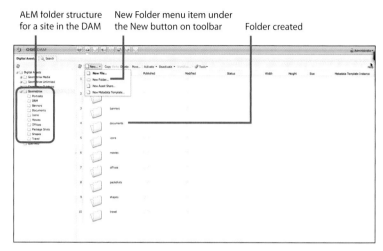

Uploading new content to DAM

4 Double-check the location of the folder within the structure to confirm it was created correctly.

How to upload and activate assets

1 On the welcome screen, click Digital Assets.

2 Navigate to the folder you'd like to add an asset to and click the New button in the DAM toolbar. Choose New File.

New button   New File menu item

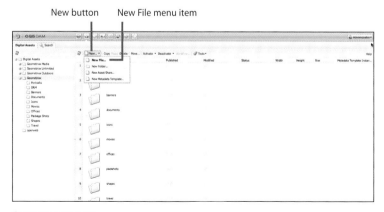

Creating a new asset

3   The system prompts you to upload a new asset. Browse to the
desired asset, or multiple assets, on a local or network machine
and select the files. Click Upload to upload all the assets to the
designated folder. Alternatively, you can also simply drag one or
more assets at once directly from your directory into the desired
DAM folder.

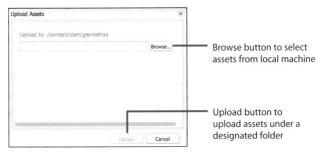

Browse button to select
assets from local machine

Upload button to
upload assets under a
designated folder

Confirm the Upload To destination is correct.

Images selected
for upload

If you need to browse to another folder for
more assets, you can do so from this dialog.

4 Once you have uploaded an asset, you can send a request to activate the asset by initiating an activation workflow (see Chapter 8).

For a publisher or an administrator, the Activate button will be enabled on the DAM toolbar. Click the Activate button and then choose Activate from the drop-down menu to activate and publish the asset immediately.

If you have permission to activate an asset, the Activate button will be enabled on the DAM toolbar.

AEM puts an appropriate pending status for that asset based on the other assets marked for activation in the queue.

Publishing status

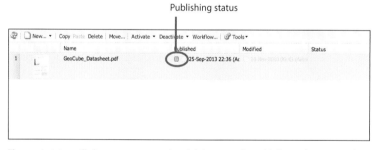

The asset status will change to orange when it is in queue for publishing. The status color will change to green once it has been successfully published.

How to delete an asset

1 Navigate to the Digital Assets interface from the AEM welcome screen. Select the asset you want to delete and click the Delete button in the DAM toolbar. You can also right-click the asset and choose Delete from the context menu.

Delete button in
DAM toolbar

Delete option in the
context menu of an asset

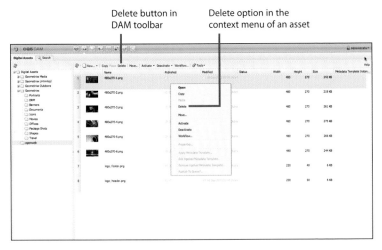

Two ways to delete an asset

The system prompts you to confirm the deletion.

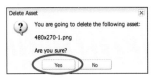

Confirm deletion prompt; if the asset has references
to other pages, the system will alert you.

2 Click Yes to initiate the asset deletion process. If the asset has no references to any pages on any site, the asset will simply be deleted from DAM. If the asset has references to other pages, the system will throw a warning prompt notifying the user.

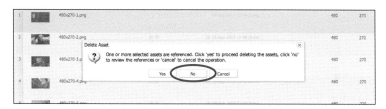

3 In the system prompt, click No to see all the references for the asset that needs to be deleted.

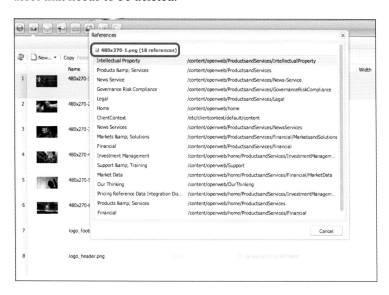

4 Alternatively, if you click the Tools button in the DAM toolbar and then choose References from the drop-down menu, you'll see all the references for a particular asset (before you initiate the deletion process).

Tools button in the   References option in the
DAM toolbar   Tools drop-down menu

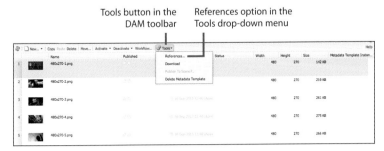

How to see all asset references

How to edit asset properties and metadata

1 Right-click the asset you want to edit and click Open from the context menu.

Right-click the asset to open a menu of actions.

A detailed asset view opens with different editable properties, including title, description, tags, language, and other fields.

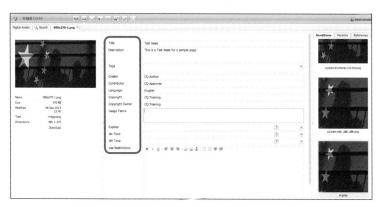

An asset's editable properties in the detailed asset view

2 In order to change the asset tags, click the Tags drop-down. To assign a tag, double-click a particular property from the tags pane.

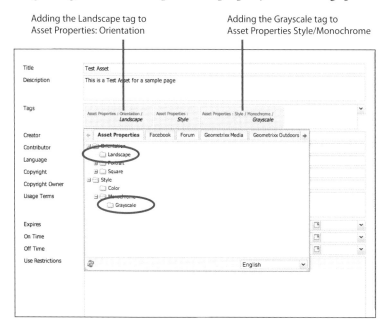

Changing an asset's tags

3 Click Save to save all the changes.

Save button

Making asset changes

How to restore an asset

From time to time, you'll need to restore an asset to a previous version. For example, if it was modified incorrectly or if its tags were changed in error, you could use the restore function to set it back to its former state.

1 Right-click the asset you'd like to edit and choose Open from the context menu.

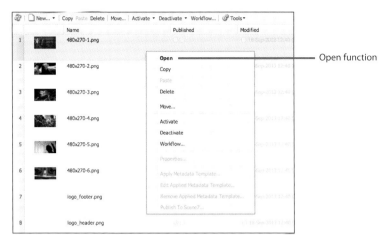

Right-click an asset to open the menu.

2 In the detailed asset view, click the Versions tab to show all the available versions for that asset.

3 Select a version and click the Restore button to set the asset to another version.

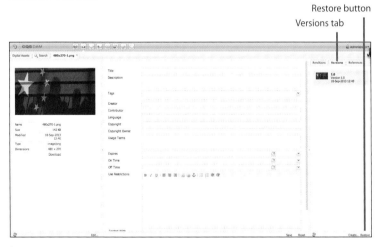

Restore an asset.

You can add a version label and comments for the new version of the image.

4 Click OK to finish.

Label the new version and add comments.

Alternatively, you can also restore an asset directly by clicking the Tools button in the DAM toolbar and choosing Restore from the drop-down menu.

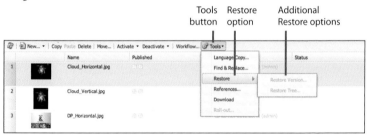

Restore feature on the toolbar

How to use DAM to transcode videos into different formats

Before enabling DAM to transcode videos, ensure that AEM framework is enabled with FFmpeg encoder add-on.

1 If you haven't already, install the FFmpeg encoder add-on from http://ffmpeg.org.

2 Unzip the Installation folder and set the system environment variable path to *<your-ffmpeg-location>*\bin.

3 Restart AEM.

Once the FFmpeg add-on has been set up, ensure that AEM has a set of Video profiles, which defines a set of video configuration properties for a particular video format, such as MP4, FLV, and so on. Configurations applied on these video profiles will enable the transcoding workflows to generate alternate video formats for a video asset.

AEM comes prebundled with some video profiles, which can be reconfigured per the transcoding needs.

4 In the AEM toolbar, click the Tools button and choose DAM > Video Profiles.

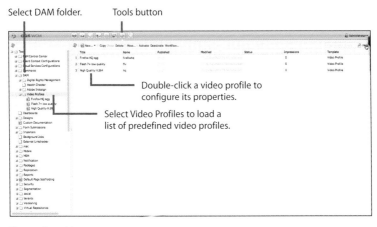

Transcoding video

5 To test out your video transcoding feature, upload a test video
   in any format other than H.264 and click Run Test. If FFmpeg
   is installed correctly, the system successfully transcodes the
   uploaded video in H.264 format.

Upload a video   Test the uploaded
from local machine.   video for transcoding.

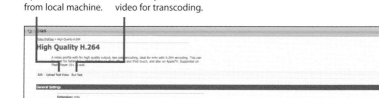

Transcoding video

6 To edit more properties of the video profile, click the Edit button
   on the Video Profiles component toolbar. In the Video Profile
   Settings dialog box, you can change various settings and naming
   conventions for the selected video profile. Click OK to save all
   changes.

Changing video profile settings

7 Once the Video profile is configured, navigate to a page in the AEM site hierarchy and add a video component.

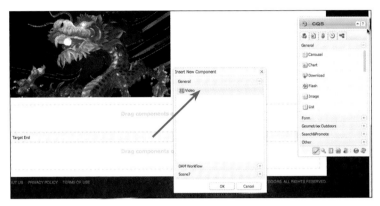

Adding a video component to a web page

8 Edit the video component to see the component's properties. On the Profiles tab, select the video profile the video should convert to while playing on this page.

Edit Component > Profiles

How to upload assets using Web DAV

1 In order to set the Web DAV, set the network drive to the following:

http://localhost:<portnumber>/crx/repository/crx.default

Setting the network drive to this path will enable the simple drag and drop feature to upload assets to CRX repository.

Set the network drive path to the CRX repository in the Server Address field.

Click Connect to set the drive.

Setting the network drive

The server prompts you to enter the credentials to connect to the AEM repository.

2 Select Registered User (Mac), or simply enter user ID and password (Windows). Click Connect to set up the repository as a drive on your local machine.

Select Registered User (Mac), or simply enter
user ID and password (Windows).

Once the repository is set up as the drive, it will be viewable from My Computer (Windows) or Finder (Mac).

CRX repository   CRX folder

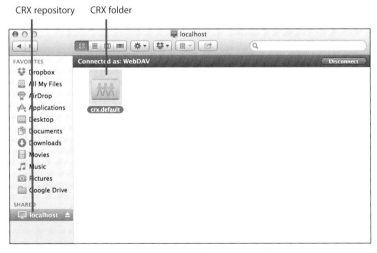

The repository is viewable in My Computer (Windows) or Finder (Mac).

3 Once inside the directory, navigate to crx.default > Content > DAM. In this directory, you can create new folders and drag and drop assets to directly import assets into DAM.

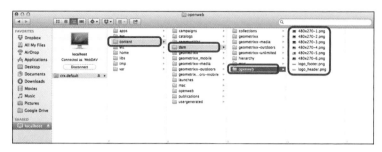

Drag and drop assets to directly import assets into DAM.

5
Tagging and Metadata

Metadata is information about data. The Dewey Decimal Classification System, which established the modern library system in the 19th century, is a great example of metadata at work. The revolutionary system categorized books by their content instead of their physical features (height and date of acquisition), thus giving people the ability to easily find books by subject. Even though the system continues to be updated, it has proven to be a fundamentally sound standard.

Metadata management is a core feature of any WEM system. It allows content to be stored, organized, and managed so it is easily found and targeted online.

The building block of metadata is the tag. Business users create tags to manage content relationships and integrations. The tags themselves have a structural relationship, but it does not have to mimic the structure of the website. In this way, tags offer the ability to categorize content using different facets of the business.

To ensure that tags are useful, authors should tag content thoroughly, completely, and accurately while using a common vocabulary. People can build very sophisticated taxonomy systems, but if they're difficult to use or navigate, they will ultimately fail.

Tag Manager

The Tag Manager is the main interface for working with tags in AEM. This interface allows you to manage your taxonomy and classification systems. From here, you can perform basic functions like creating, editing, deleting, and moving tags.

Tagging tree hierarchy: Expand or collapse the navigation tree.

Quick links to other AEM features provide a global navigation to core management interfaces.

The toolbar for tag management operations: create, read, update, and delete tags.

Search by keyword to find tags.

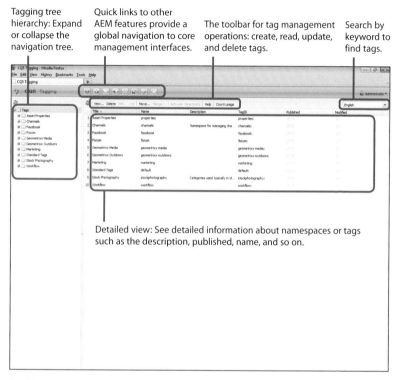

Detailed view: See detailed information about namespaces or tags such as the description, published, name, and so on.

Tag Manager

Working with tags

Tags possess their own hierarchical structure and relationships, all of which can be managed in the Tag Manager.

How to create tag namespaces

A namespace is a logical grouping of tags by subject or application. The same tag may appear in different namespaces, but always create a namespace first before associating tags to it.

1   On the AEM welcome screen, click Tagging.

2   In the Tag Manager, select the Tags folder and click the New button to create a new namespace.

The tag folder displays
all namespaces, or   Click the New button to
groupings, of tags.   create a new namespace.

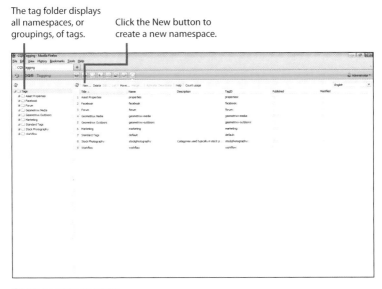

Creating a new namespace

3   Enter a title, name, and description for the new namespace and click Create.

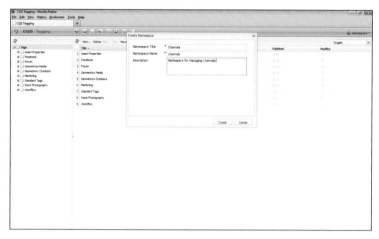

The Create Namespace dialog box allows you to define all information about a namespace.

How to create a tag

Tags work as the glue between content relationships. Keep these relationships in mind when you are creating tags in AEM.

1   In the Tag Manager, select the namespace where you want to create a new tag. Click New.

Selected namespace   New button

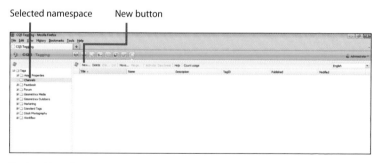

Tag tree hierarchy

2 Enter title, name, and description for the new tag and click Create.

Create Tag dialog box

TIP ▶ Do not create tags or namespaces that will only be used on a single page. Instead, focus on tags that are reusable. You can define a unique tag for a page in page details, which is covered in the next section.

How to associate a tag with a page

Now that you've created a tag, you'll need to associate it with a page.

1 On the AEM welcome screen, open the Websites interface.

2 In the website tree hierarchy, double-click the page you want to associate with the tags.

Page to associate tags

Website interface

3 When the page loads in edit mode, open the Page tab (second tab) of the sidekick.

4 Click Page Properties to open the Page Properties dialog box.

Page Properties link in the Sidekick

5 In the Tags/Keywords field, start typing the tag to associate with the page. As you type, suggested tags will appear in a drop-down list.

Tags/Keywords field

Page Properties dialog box

6 From the suggested list of tags, select the tag you want to associate with the page. If you want to create a unique tag not already in Tag Manager and associate it with the page, you can just type it in. Alternatively, you can press the down arrow on the right side of the tag/keyword textbox to get a full list of namespaces with associated tags that you can select from.

Tag suggestions

7 Click OK to save the tag association.

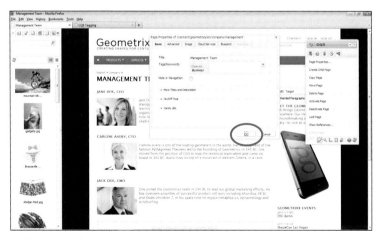

Click OK to save changes.

How to edit/move/delete tags

There will come a time when you want to move, edit, or delete a tag. If your product name changes, for example, you can remove that tag from the Tag Manager to remove it from all the pages it's associated with.

HOW TO EDIT A TAG

1 On the AEM welcome screen, click Tagging.
2 Select the namespace where the tag is saved and select the tag to be edited from the list of tags on the right.
3 In the toolbar, click the Edit button.

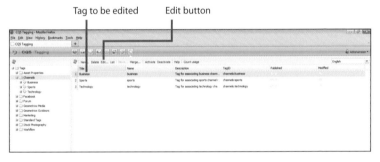

Tag Manager

4 In the Edit dialog box, make the changes, and click Save.

Edit Tag dialog box

TIP ► Use the Description field to add information that describes the tag. For example, if you use the word Java, the description could specify whether it refers to the development language or coffee. Descriptions give the tag context.

HOW TO MOVE A TAG

1 On the AEM welcome screen, click Tagging.

2 Select the namespace where the tag is stored. Select the tag to be moved from the list of tags on the right.

3 In the toolbar, click the Move button.

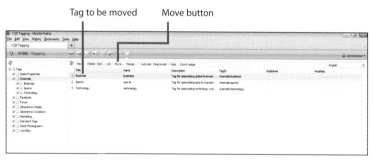

Tag Manager

4 In the Move Tag dialog box, click the path selector button to open the Select Path dialog box.

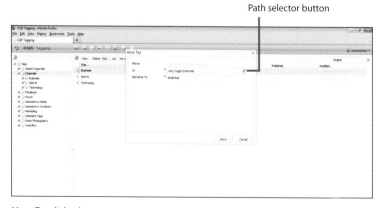

Move Tag dialog box

5   Select the target path where you want to move the tag, and then
click OK.

Select Path dialog box

6   Click the Move button to move the tag to the new location.

Move button

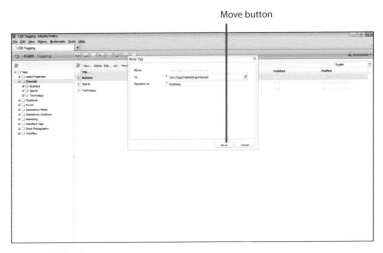

Move Tag dialog box

7 Navigate to the new location to confirm that the tag has been moved.

New location for tag

HOW TO DELETE A TAG

1 Navigate to Tagging from the AEM welcome screen.

2 Select the namespace where the tag is saved. Select the tag to be deleted from the list on the right.

3 In the toolbar, click the Delete button.

Tag to be deleted   Delete button

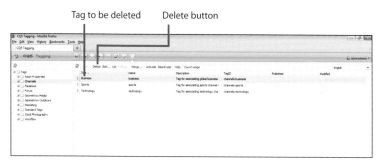

Tag Manager

4 Click Yes to confirm the deletion.

Yes button confirms tag deletion

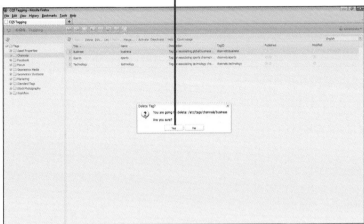

Confirm deletion dialog box

TIP ▶ When you delete a tag it will remove its association with webpages.

6

Personalization

One of AEM's most powerful features is the ability to create personalized content for specific segments or groups of site visitors, or to test variations of content for optimization. AEM's robust framework handles these strategies seamlessly and allows you to create compelling, engaging content to all users.

Working with user profiles

AEM's user profiles can target campaigns and content to specific visitor segments based on common attributes such as age, gender, location, browser type, lifestyle, and so on. First, begin by learning how to create a user, and then you will learn how to personalize or target content in AEM to this user.

How to create user profiles in AEM

1   On the AEM welcome screen, click Users. You can also get to the Security console by clicking the Users icon from other AEM interfaces.

2   In the Security console, click Edit > Create > Create User.

3 Enter user information into the required fields and click Create.

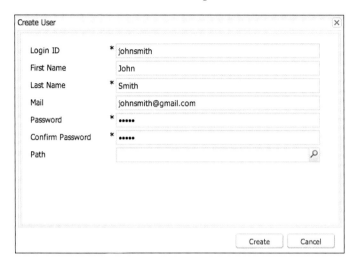

4 Search for the newly created user in the search box, and then double-click the user ID to see detailed information.

Search for the new user to confirm   Click the user to
the user was successfully created.   see details.

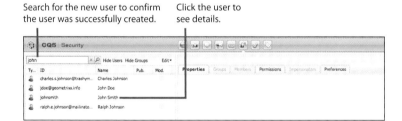

Personalizing content

Once you've identified specific user groups, you may want to create unique experiences for them through personalization.

How to personalize content based on visitor traits

1   Navigate to the specific page you want to manage in the Websites interface. In the Sidekick, click the Client Context icon.

    This example uses the Geometrixx site to illustrate this concept.

Client Context icon

TIP ▶ The Client Context is your go-to tool for authoring dynamic content, enabling you to simulate different site visitors, their geographic locations, and their browser or device types, as well as to simulate campaigns and segments. Its window floats above your authoring experience, similar to the Sidekick. It's not there by default, but you can open it from the Sidekick.

2 Click the Load icon to load a profile in the Client Context.

Load a profile in the Client Context.

3 In the Profile Loader dialog box, select the user you created and click OK.

User to base the profile on

Once a user has been selected, you can edit a number of user traits directly within the interface.

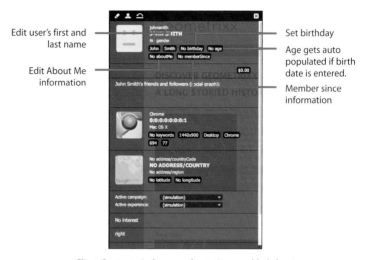

Edit user's first and last name

Edit About Me information

Set birthday

Age gets auto populated if birth date is entered.

Member since information

Client Context window; as other traits are added about a user they will also appear in this window.

4   In order to add more profile data, click the Edit icon in the Client Context window.

Edit icon

The Client Context window opens in edit mode, where you can edit each individual component and add more fields.

5   To add/edit more traits, right-click the first component and
    choose Edit from the context menu.

Profile Data dialog box

Based on the selected traits, you can now select different
active campaigns/segments to showcase for that profile on
that particular page.

Select an active campaign for summer for Gender=Male and Age> 30.

Click Experiences to see a list of segments available

Select the appropriate segment to showcase
on the site for that particular profile.

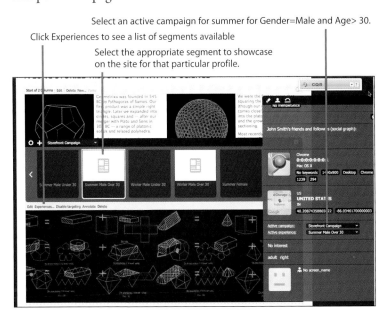

How to personalize content based on location

Targeting website content based on a visitor's location is a powerful and easy way to create a personalized experience. Regional trends and seasonal changes are just two areas to consider.

1   Navigate to the specific page you want to personalize by location, and click the Client Context icon in the Sidekick.

2   Click the map interface and select a location by dropping the location pin on the map.

Click the map graphic to drop a pin
on the desired location.

Client Context will update the location and will also set the specific coordinates.

Update location

Select the desired campaign and experience.

Select the targeted experience
to display on the particular page.

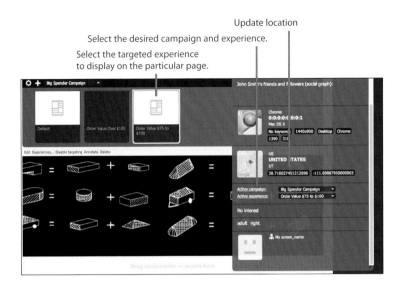

How to personalize content based on technology

Personalizing based on browser or device type will help you deliver
the best user experience based on the parameters of the technology,
such as screen size, support for Flash, and so on.

In order to personalize content based on a particular browser, it's
assumed you've created a segment for specific browser names.
(Refer to Chapter 11 for detailed information about creating segments and campaigns.)

1   Once a segment has been created, you can assign that particular segment to a campaign or experience and add relevant content to display when the browser type matches.

In the toolbar, click the Campaigns button.

Select the desired campaign from the Campaigns list.

Create a new experience by clicking the New button.

Assign the segment created in previous screen to this experience.

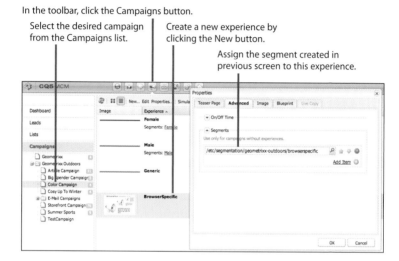

2   In the Sidekick, click the Client Context icon and navigate to the profile. Click the Load icon to load a profile in the Client Context.

Load a profile.

3 Select the campaign for a specific browser type from the Active Campaign and Active Experience drop-down menus. On the page, edit the experience component and select the desired segment type to display the attached content.

Once you change parameters in the Client Context, the page should change as it personalizes content based on the traits you've selected. Occasionally you will need to refresh the page if you don't see the changes your expecting.

7

Multi-site Manager, Internationalization, and Content Reuse

Your website is the global face of your organization, potentially opening up your customer base to countries around the world. As a result, you should be prepared to meet your users where they are—not just digitally, but linguistically and culturally as well. AEM provides tools that make it easier to create multilingual content, to rapidly develop sites, and manage content across sites.

Multi-site Manager

Adobe's Multi-site Manager (MSM) turns a tedious manual process into an automated process that maximizes consistency throughout multiple sites. MSM allows you to define relationships between sites and control which assets you want to reuse.

Its benefits include the following:

- Maintain a common look and feel between sites
- Localize content or determine what content shows up (or doesn't) for country sites
- Manage relationships between sites and content to encourage reuse

Multi-site Manager will require the help of your IT team, and this chapter provides important concepts to help you communicate with them.

How to create a blueprint

A blueprint is used to define the structure you want to use as a source website for one or more Live Copy pages.

1 From the AEM home page, click the Tools link. You can also access the Tools interface via the icon on the AEM toolbar.

Tools icon

2 Select MSM Control Center, which will list out the available blueprints in AEM.

Click MSM Control Center to view available blueprints.

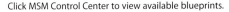
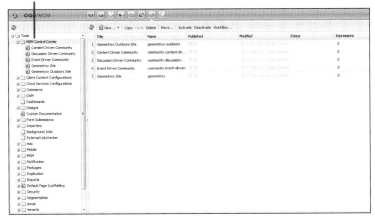

3 Click the New button and choose New Page from the drop-down menu.

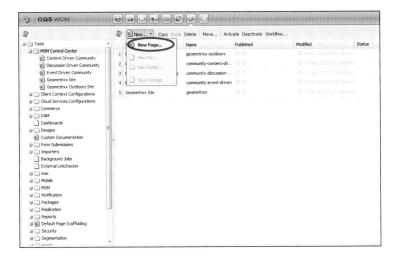

4 Enter the title and name of the new blueprint and select the Blueprint Template. Click Create.

5 Open the new blueprint's settings by double-clicking its name.

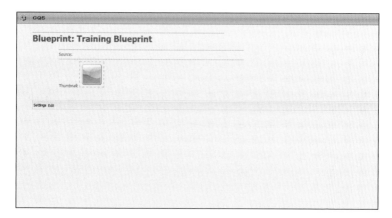

6 Click the Edit button to configure the blueprint and provide the blueprint description and source path. It's suggested you also provide the thumbnail image.

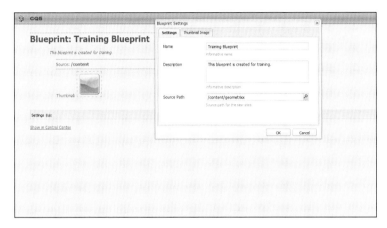

For easier reference, include a thumbprint image in the blueprint settings, which will work as a visual cue for content authors.

How to create a live copy

1 From the AEM home page, click the Websites link. If you're in another interface, just click the Websites icon on the AEM toolbar.

Websites interface

2   Click New on the toolbar and choose New Site from the drop-down menu.

3   Enter the title and name of the website and select the Blueprint Template. Click Next.

4   Select the preferred language and click Next.

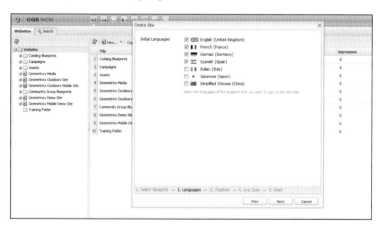

5   Select the initial chapters and click Next.

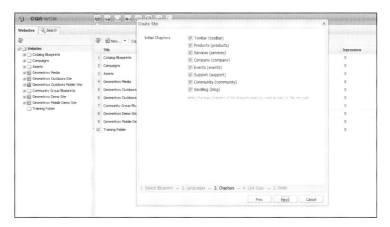

6   For Site Owner, choose the existing user and deselect the Live Copy option. For Rollout Configs, choose Standard Rollout Config. Click Next.

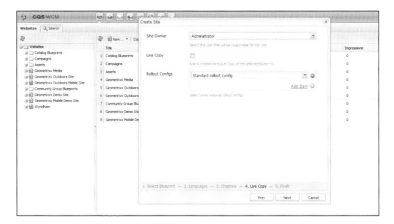

7 Click Create Site.

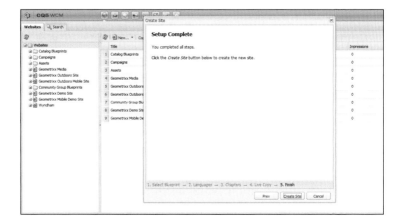

The new blueprint site is now available in the website listing.

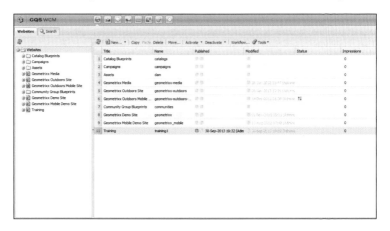

How to select a rollout configuration

With the use of a blueprint, an exact replica of the site can be developed, which will be referred to as Live Copy. It's helpful in reducing the overall development effort, but it doesn't cover the entire process. In most cases you'll need to change the template and resource types of your Live Copy pages. These changes can be made using rollout configurations in Live Copy. With a rollout configuration, AEM automatically creates a new page in the other website any time you create a new page in your main site, taking the exact content from the new main page while still using the second site's designs.

To find rollout configurations, navigate to the node etc/msm/rolloutconfigs in the CRX Explorer. Here, you'll find out-of-the-box configurations files as well as some custom Geometrixx configurations. You can create new rollout configurations from scratch or by copying an existing layout and altering it to your project's needs.

The Trigger property tells AEM when to use specific configurations. You can specify that a particular configuration be used only on a site's initial rollout.

There are four types of triggers:
- Rollout (performed when a page is rolled out)
- Modification (performed when a page is modified)
- Publish (performed when a page is activated)
- Deactivation (performed when a page is deactivated)

INSTALLED ROLLOUT CONFIGURATIONS

The following rollout configurations are installed by default.

Table 7.1 Installed rollout configurations

CONFIGURATION NAME	EVENT ON THE SOURCE PAGE THAT TRIGGERS THE ACTION	PERFORMED ACTIONS ON THE LIVE COPY
Standard rollout configuration	On Rollout	Content Update Content Copy Content Delete References Update Order Children
Activate on blueprint activation	On Activation	Target Activate
Deactivate on blueprint deactivation	On Deactivation	Target Deactivate
Push on modify	On Modification	Content Update Content Copy Content Delete References Update Order Children
Geometrixx Mobile	On Rollout	Content Update Content Copy Content Delete Edit Properties References Update Order Children
Geometrixx Outdoors Mobile	On Rollout	Edit Properties
Geometrixx Outdoors Mobile Teaser	On Rollout	Edit Properties

Creating translated copy

AEM facilitates an automated process to manage multilingual content. It provides a translation workflow, which enables the user to copy content from a source site tree in one language into a different language tree. Then, the user can translate pages of that new tree using a workflow review process—or integrate this translation workflow with an external translation application during this step. A side-by-side view, as well as versioning of the old source page, is also included.

As a prerequisite, you must have set up a site in the following structure:

- The root level contains the name of your website
- The following children contain names reflecting the different language roots. You need at least two children—one source language to be translated from, and at least one destination language to be translated into. Those child page language names must conform to the ISO naming convention for languages, for instance "en" for English, and so on. This naming convention is detailed here: http://dev.day.com/docs/en/cq/current/administering/multi_site_manager.html#Adding a new language version
- The content pages of each language site is located underneath its respective language parent, specified in the step above.

How to use MSM to manage language-specific versions

1 From the AEM home page, click the Websites link. If you're in another interface, just click the Websites icon on the AEM toolbar.

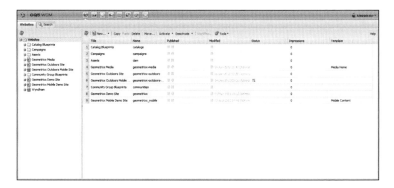

2 From the Websites console, select the root page of the website.

3 Create a new child page within the root page of the website. This page will represent the new language version of the website.

4 Click the New button and choose New Page from the drop-down menu.

5 Use the language name for the page title. Use the language code for the page name. Select a template from the list and click Create.

6 Select the root page of the website.

7 Click the Tools button and choose Language Copy from the drop-down menu.

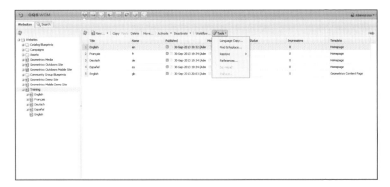

The Language Copy dialog box displays a matrix of available language versions and webpages. An X in a language column means that the page is available in that language.

8 To copy an existing page or page tree to a language version, select the cell for that page in the language column.

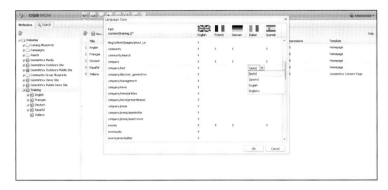

9 Select the language from which content needs to be copied.

10 Click OK and then click Yes to confirm.

11 Confirm that the new language page is now under the website listing. You will find the page under the new language website.

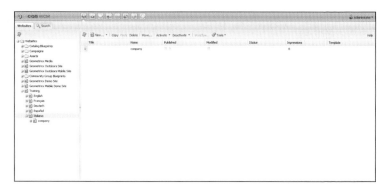

How to set tag translations

With AEM, you can translate tags into different languages. Tag titles
can then be localized either according to the user language or to the
page language.

1 From the AEM home page, click the Tools link.

AEM home page (mobile user interface)

2   Click Tag Management.

Click Tag Management link

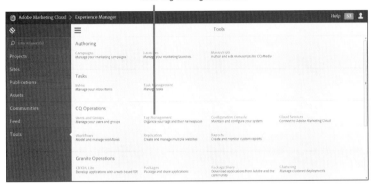

Tag Management link

All tags in their respective folders are visible in the Tag Management interface.

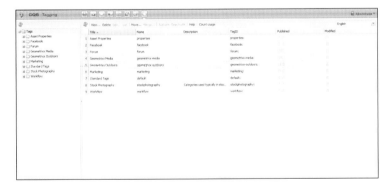

3 Select the tag you want made available in different languages. Right-click the tag and choose Edit from the context menu.

Right-click menu on tag

4 Provide the language translations for the given tag and click Save.

Edit tag dialog box

Each user in AEM can set his preferred language, which is applied to tags as well as content. In the example above, a user who has set German as the preferred language will see *platz* as the tag rather than *square*.

5 Applying the translated tag to a page requires you to navigate to the Websites interface. To do this, click Websites icon and navigate to the desired page.

6 Select the page. Right-click it and choose Properties from the context menu.

7 In Tags/Keywords, click the selection arrow bar to highlight the tag hierarchy. Select the language to automatically select the translated tags.

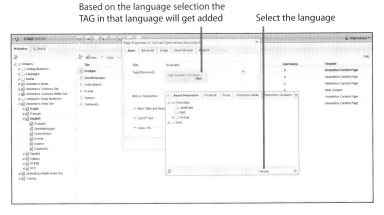

Adding a translated tag to the Page properties

8 Click Save to add the tag to the Page Properties.

How to initiate translation workflow

1   From the AEM home page, click Websites to open the Websites interface.

2   Create a new page under the source language (such as English). In this example, a new page called Testpage is created under Geometrixx > English.

Create a new page under the source language root.

3   Open up the newly created page in edit mode. In the Sidekick, click the Workflow tab.

4   Expand the Sidekick's translation section. Select the language this page should be translated into.

5   Select Workflow Translation and click Translate to create a duplicate page in the selected language section. In this example, Testpage was created under the German folder.

Translate button activates the Translation workflow

Translating the page using Sidekick's Translation workflow

NOTE ▶ The grayed-out languages mean that the page does not exist under that language tree yet. If the language is not grayed out, this page previously exists.

6 Activate the source page in English by clicking Activate Page in the Sidekick's Page Properties tab.

This creates a new version of the page in its appropriate language folder.

Activate source page to create a new version of it.

NOTE ▶ The version of the page can now also be seen in crxdelight. The page has a jcr:mixinTypes = mix:versionable property.

7 Open up the translated page under the new language folder. Go to the Workflow tab in the Sidekick. Here you'll see the translated (newly copied) page is under workflow (and the workflow has not been completed yet).

The translation workflow of the newly translated page

8 Expand the Translation tab to show the version of the reference page—in this case the Testpage under English.

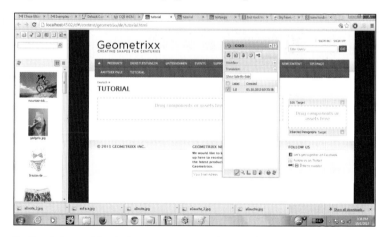

The Translation workflow in the new page copy is shown under the new language folder.

9 Click the Show Side-By-Side button to show the difference between the original page and the new page, which is to be translated. On the left, translate the page into the target language. This example uses German.

Show Side-By-Side feature compares both versions of the page

10 To illustrate this process better, go back to the source page under EN. Add some content. Activate the page again to create a new version of it.

Add new content to the original source page and re-activate it to see the workflow in action.

11 Go back to the target page under the translated language. In this example, it's DE. Go to the Sidekick Workflow tab and select the newest version and click Show Side-By-Side. The new content shows up on the right in the source page tab.

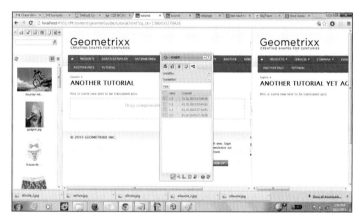

Modified content in side-by-side view

TIP ▶ You can see in the Workflow inbox that the translated pages are indeed under Workflow. This is another way of opening up the newly created page under the new language tree.

For this, go to http://localhost:4502/inbox to see the Workflow inbox. Double-click the content to open up the translated page.

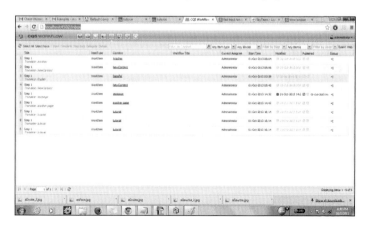

See the newly copied pages to be translated in the Workflow inbox.

TIP ► You can create a Workflow Process step in this out-of-the-box Translation workflow, for instance to integrate with a third-party provider to automate the translation step itself. The Translation Workflow Model as it comes out of the box can be accessed from the Workflow console and edited under http://localhost:4502/cf#/etc/workflow/models/translation.html.

Content inheritance

You can inherit in AEM different ways—the following sections are some examples for how to set content for reuse.

How to use a reference component

1   Open the Websites interface from the AEM home page, and double-click the webpage to open it in edit mode.

2   On a page, drag the out-of-the-box Reference component into the desired paragraph system. The Reference component is located under the General section of the Sidekick.

Reference component in the Sidekick

3 Double-click the Reference component. Enter a path to the content of a page. Select the drop-down menu, which opens up a navigator to all the pages in your content tree. It is easier in most cases to type the path of the content you would like to reference.

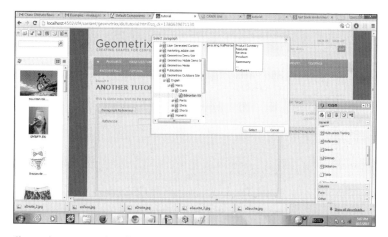

Choose the content to be referenced from the site tree navigator of the component.

NOTE ▶ You can reference entire paragraphs, a single text node on a paragraph, or dialog nodes.

Choose the content to be referenced by typing the path to a node.

4   Update the original component's content. In this example, the
title of the page will be updated.

Updating the original content for the Reference component.

5   Refresh the page with the reference component on it. You will see
that the content is updated here, too. In this example, the title is
updated.

Updated content appears inside the Reference component after a page refresh.

How to break inheritance

When editing a component, if you notice you can't edit it and it is locked, the content is being inherited.

1   To break the inheritance, click the lock. You are prompted to ensure you want to break inheritance.

2   Click OK.

This allows you to edit the content directly versus receiving updates from the source. You can revert back to inheritance by clicking the lock again.

Click the lock to break inheritance

8
Workflows

Workflows automate processes and create efficiencies within a content management system. Adobe Experience Manager provides ready-made workflows as well as the ability to create custom workflows, depending on your needs. (Although keep in mind that creating workflows will typically be an IT team task.) Even small teams will find workflows helpful in moving content through the creation and approval process.

Using inbox for workflow tasks

Inbox can be used to manage the workflow steps to activate, approve, and publish content.

How to activate content

1   In Site Admin, select the website you want to work with from the website hierarchy on the left. From here, you can either:

   • Right-click the page you want to work with from the page hierarchy and choose Workflow from the context menu.

   • In the toolbar, click the Workflow button.

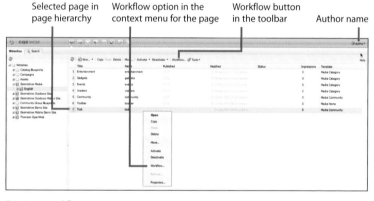

Starting a workflow

2 In the Start Workflow dialog box, choose "Request for Activation" and click Start to send the content to the designated approver's inbox.

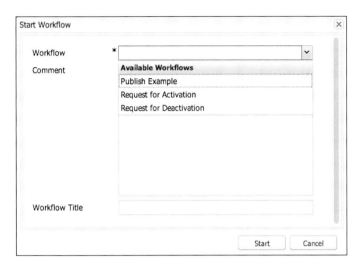

How to approve content

1 Log in as an approver or administrator in AEM and click the Inbox icon on the Site Admin toolbar. On the Inbox toolbar, click the Complete button (or right-click the content activation request and choose Complete from the context menu).

Inbox icon in the main toolbar

Complete button in
the inbox toolbar

Complete option in the
context menu

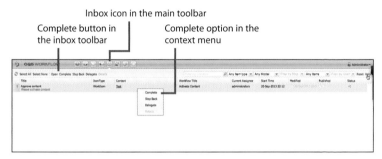

Using right-click to approve content

2 In the Complete Workflow dialog box, choose "Request for activation," add any relevant comments, and click OK.

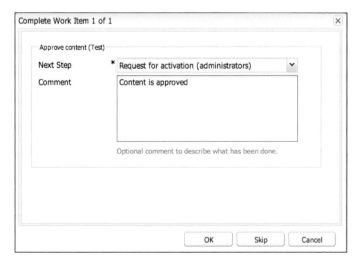

The comments will vary based on what content type is being sent for activation and whom it is being sent to.

How to publish content

1   Log in as an administrator or publisher and go to AEM inbox. On the Inbox toolbar, click the Complete button (or right-click the approved content workflow step and choose Complete from the context menu).

2   In the dialog box, choose Activate Page and click OK to activate and publish the content.

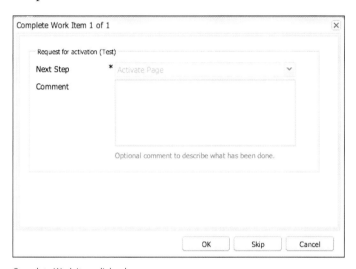

Complete Work Item dialog box

Managing a workflow from an asset

In AEM, a workflow process can be started directly from a page by using the Workflow menu in the AEM Sidekick, eliminating the need to go back to the inbox between steps.

How to manage workflow functions directly from an asset

1 From the AEM welcome screen, click Websites. In the website hierarchy on the left, double-click the page you want to activate.

Select the page to be activated

2 From the content page, click the Workflow icon in the Sidekick. Choose "Request for Activation" from the drop-down menu. Click the Start Workflow button to initiate the workflow process.

Initiating workflow from an asset

3 Log in as an approver or administrator and navigate to the same page either from the administrator inbox or via the Websites page hierarchy. From the Sidekick, choose Approve Content from the drop-down menu and click Complete.

Approve content from the Sidekick

4 Log in as a publisher or administrator and choose Request For Activation from the drop-down menu and click Complete to activate/publish the content.

Request for activation from the Sidekick

Other Features

AEM's other workflow features include annotating content and creating a custom workflow.

How to annotate content

Annotations provide an easy way to communicate comments and feedback on content. They are better than just leaving comments in the workflow process because they provide a visual representation of the changes needed before the content is activated. Annotations are made after the author has submitted a request for activation to approver/administrator.

1 Log in as an approver or administrator and click Inbox (either from the AEM welcome screen or on the AEM toolbar).

2 In the Content column, click the page name to visit the page you want to activate.

Inbox icon   Page name to be reviewed and annotated

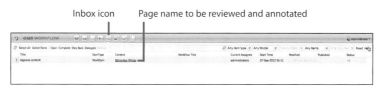

Select the content to be approved.

3 To add an annotation, right-click a component and choose Annotate from the context menu.

Annotate option in the component context menu

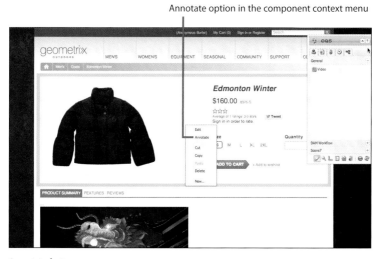

Annotate feature

4   Enter comments in the comment box, which will be saved automatically.

Comments will be saved automatically and visible to other users.

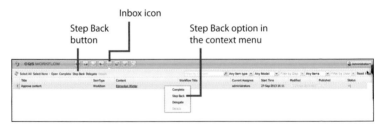

Annotation within the component

TIP ▶ To delete a comment, click the X icon on the top right of the comment box. When the content is activated, any remaining comments are deleted automatically.

5   Go back to the Inbox and click the Step Back button, or right-click the inbox task and choose Step Back from the context menu, to send the task to the last process in the workflow, such as back to the author's inbox.

Inbox icon

Step Back button

Step Back option in the context menu

Step Back feature

How to create a workflow

Workflow creation is a powerful AEM utility that allows advanced AEM users and developers to create custom workflows to suit their business needs. This feature is generally used by the IT department and not casual business users.

1   To create a simple workflow, click the Tools icon on the AEM toolbar (or on the welcome screen). Open the Workflow folder.

Tools icon

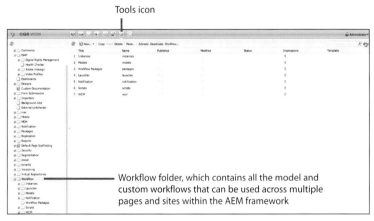

Workflow folder, which contains all the model and custom workflows that can be used across multiple pages and sites within the AEM framework

Tools interface

2 On the workflow toolbar, choose New Page from the drop-down menu to create a new workflow model.

New button in the
workflow toolbar

Choosing New Page will allow users to create a new
workflow model from a workflow model template.

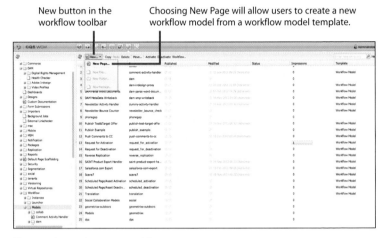

First steps in creating a new workflow

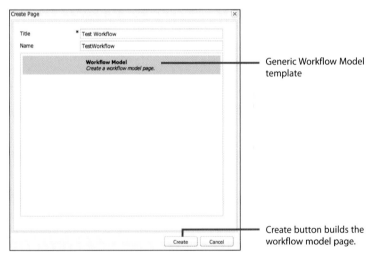

Generic Workflow Model
template

Create button builds the
workflow model page.

New workflow

3   Click Create to create the workflow model in the page hierarchy. Right-click the workflow model you just created and choose Open from the context menu.

Workflow model created   Open to modify the
in the page hierarchy   workflow model

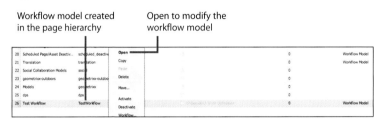

Right-click the newly created workflow

You can now edit the workflow steps, assigned authors, and events for the workflow.

4   To add a new workflow step, simply drag and drop the step from the Sidekick to the flowchart.

List of users and groups set up in the AEM

First step identifies which audience has access to the workflow. In this example the workflow is meant only for administrators. A different user/user-group can be added to this by simply dragging and dropping to this component.

Save button saves   Drag and drop a workflow step
all the changes.   from Sidekick to the flowchart.

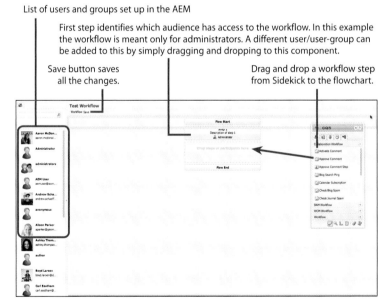

Workflow audience, features, and steps

When a workflow step is added to the flow, the workflow will be updated with the new step.

Activate Page step for administrators has been added.

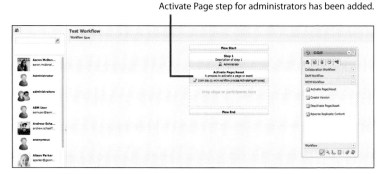

Updated workflow with new steps added

5 To confirm your workflow was completed successfully, navigate to the AEM Websites page hierarchy as an administrator. Select a page and click the Workflow button on the page toolbar.

Your new workflow appears in the drop-down menu.

Workflow button

New workflow appears in the drop-down for administrators.

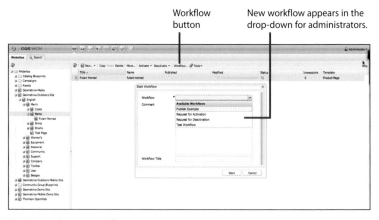

Testing out the new workflow

9

Mobile

Authoring a site for mobile devices involves many of the same steps as a website, but with a few extra considerations. There are thousands of mobile devices on the market, each with different screen sizes, technologies, and other subtle nuances. Supporting the mobile web or a mobile app is not trivial, but AEM provides the capabilities to do it. This chapter investigates the ways in which AEM manages mobile websites and mobile apps.

How to create a mobile site

1 From the AEM home page, click Websites (or click the Websites icon from the AEM Toolbar).

2 Click the New button on the toolbar and choose New Site from the drop-down menu.

Websites console

3 Enter a title and name. Select the Mobile template and click Create.

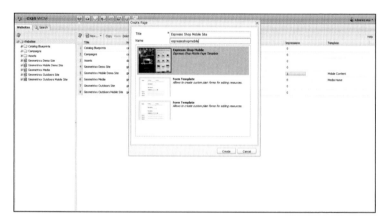

Create Page dialog box

The new mobile site appears in the list on the left.

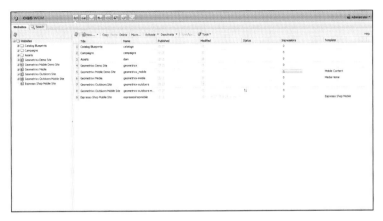

New mobile page is displayed

4 Create the language node for English content by creating a new page and labeling it with the language.

New page with language specific title and name

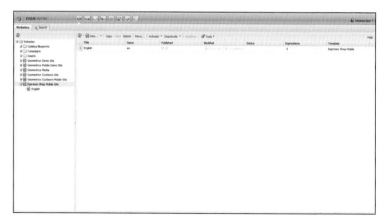

The website's pages are listed as they're created.

5 Follow the same process to create the rest of the site's pages.

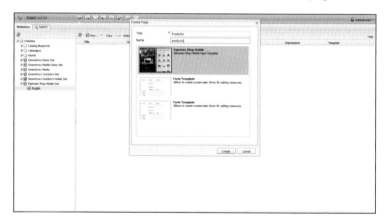

Create a new page. You will create the structure of the rest of the mobile website using mobile templates.

How to enable mobile device detection and targeting

1 On the Websites interface, navigate to the desired page and open it in Edit mode.

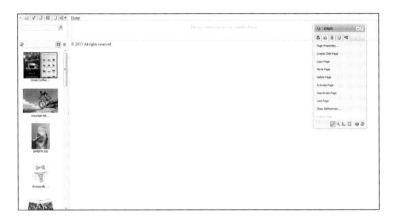

2 In the Sidekick, select Page Properties. Click the Advanced tab.

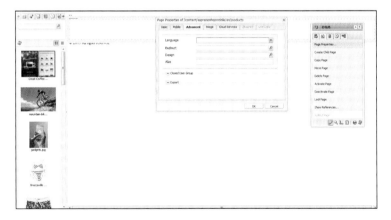

Select the Page tab in the Sidekick, then select the Page Properties > Advanced tab.

3 Select the design to apply the site-specific styles on the page.

Select design to apply to new page.

4 Click the Mobile tab to enable device groups for the page.

5 After selecting the device groups, click OK to apply the changes.

The page renders in the mobile emulator view.

How to view and edit content in the mobile emulator

AEM provides support for emulators to view mobile webpages as they would be rendered in mobile devices.

NOTE ▶ The mobile authoring interface is simply an aid to help you visualize your content experience on phones and tablets. It is not a replacement for legitimate cross-browser, cross-device testing.

Add component to a page

NOTE ▶ Because you've told AEM it's a mobile page, only the mobile components will show in the emulator.

1   To add content onto a page, do one of the following:

  • Double-click an editable area.

  • Right-click and choose New from the context menu.

  • Drag a component from the Sidekick onto an editable region.

2 Edit the content of the component by double-clicking it or by right-clicking it and choosing Edit from the context menu.

Displaying a mobile page

NOTE ▶ Once you've updated your mobile page with content, you can see how it looks in different emulators.

3 To view how the page looks in different emulators, click the Edit button at the bottom of the Sidekick. Select from the list of different mobile devices, or use the mobile device carousel at the top of the screen.

The page refreshes with an emulator of the selected device.

This shows the look of the selected HTC emulator.

Responsive testing

If you elect to implement a responsive website (a website that adapts to screen size), AEM provides a tool for testing your layout. Its function is similar to the device targeting emulator, but is more focused on screen resolution than device type. In preview mode, you can change the relative screen resolution within the Sidekick.

1 In the Sidekick, select Preview mode (the magnifying glass icon).

2 Select Desktop.

Responsive design—Desktop view

3 To see what the responsive design website would look like on a phone, select iPhone.

1. Select the device.

2. Click Rotate to see what it would look like in landscape mode.

3. The current screen resolution appears in the preview mode. In this example you can see the current resolution is 640 x 960.

Responsive design—iPhone

NOTE ▶ Once you switch to an iPhone view, you can see the website layout changes compared to the desktop view.

TIP ▶ You can cheat by selecting the edge of your browser and shrinking the browser width to the size you want to test. The responsive design format updates automatically.

How to synchronize content from your desktop site to your mobile sites

1 From the AEM home page, open the Websites interface. Click the New button on the toolbar and choose New Live Copy from the drop-down menu.

2 Enter the title and name of your mobile site, and select the source site for creating the live copy.

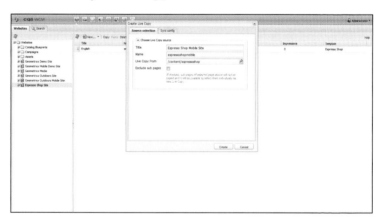

3 Click the Sync Config tab, and select the Rollout Configs option for the mobile site.

In layman's terms this is a set of instructions that tell AEM how to sync files from the desktop or web version to the mobile version. For example, when you edit content on your homepage it can automatically update the mobile website's home page as well.

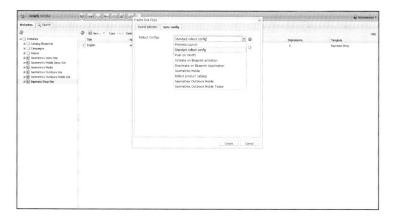

A new mobile site is created from the original site.

4 Click the Tools icon, and select the MSM Control Center.

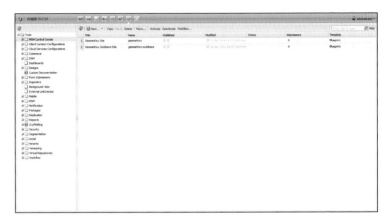

Mobile site pages can be synchronized from the MSM Control Center.

PhoneGap integration

PhoneGap is the Adobe Experience Manager solution for implementing mobile applications, such as those you download from the iTunes Store or Google Play. It's a platform that enables you to build your mobile app almost as you would a website. PhoneGap turns your website code into a program that iOS or Android devices can execute natively (without a web browser). The value in the platform is that you can write a mobile app one time, and then deploy it to multiple mobile platforms. You don't have to write separate iOS and Android applications, which can be expensive.

10

Social Communities

No longer are social features a unique differentiator for websites. Today, visitors expect to be able to read product reviews and ratings, leave comments, and skip complicated login procedures. Adobe Experience Manager provides a set of components and features so you can build social functionality into your website.

It's rare that you'll use every one of them on the same site, which would likely be too overwhelming for visitors, but you should view the AEM social features as effective tools to enable your strategy.

The benefits of social content include:

- Engages users and encourages them to spend more time on your site
- Is deemed three times more trusted, as it's generated by other users
- Allows visitors to discover user-generated content through search engines to find your website

Social Communities

The social communities feature unifies all social networking and collaboration applications with AEM.

NOTE ▶ User-generated content (UGC) is any content that is submitted by an external site visitor, most often done anonymously. Managing UCC adds an extra layer of complexity. Some of the components described in this section enable your site's visitors to create user-generated content.

How to add social components to the Sidekick

1   From the Websites interface, double-click a page you want to edit. Enter the design mode through the Sidekick, and then click Edit on a paragraph system to which you want to add a social component.

The Parsys interface appears, where you can activate components for a page.

2   Scroll to the Social Collaboration section and enable the components you want available for that content region.

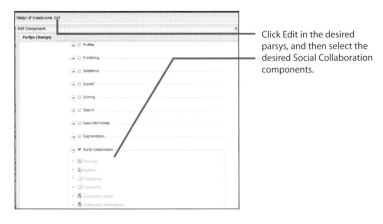

Click Edit in the desired parsys, and then select the desired Social Collaboration components.

NOTE ▶ You can enable all components in a section by selecting the section check box, or you can just select individual components.

Comments component

The comments component is key social feature that lets users share reviews, thoughts and ideas. In AEM's out-of-box comment component you can configure and control the way comments are displayed.

How to set up a comment component

1   On the Websites interface, navigate to the page you'd like to work with and double-click to open it in edit mode. Select the Comments component from the Sidekick and drag it to the content area.

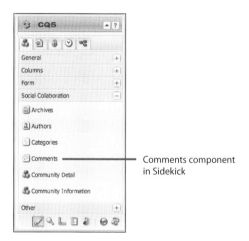

Comments component
in Sidekick

2 Configure the component using the Comments tab.

This feature will be important in formatting the date, disabling or closing the comments section, and enabling moderation.

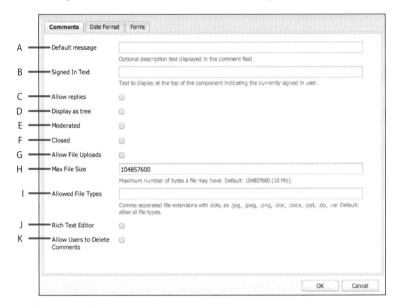

Comments settings

A. Default message: Default message for anonymous user to see

B. Signed In Text: Text to display for signed-in user

C. Allow replies: Allows replies to comments

D. Display as tree: Display comment format

E. Moderation: Enables the comment to be moderated

F. Closed: Comments are disabled and/or existing comments are closed.

G. Allow File Uploads: Allows users to upload files

H. Max File Size: Sets the max file size for uploads

I. Allowed File Types: File types that are allowed to be uploaded

J. Rich Text Editor: Lets the user to do basic formatting like bold, italic, and underline

K. Allow Users to Delete Comments: Allows users to delete their comments or replies

How to approve a comment

1 From the Websites interface, navigate to the page you'd like to moderate. Double-click the comment.

2 A moderator can select the Approve By Moderator or Mark as Spam options. More detailed moderation can be performed in AEM by navigation to http://localhost:4502/communities.html.

For custom moderation, the admin can create a custom workflow for moderation.

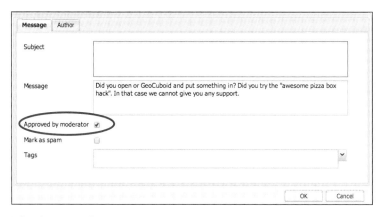

Select the Approved By Moderator option to approve the comment

How to change the date display format

1 From the Websites interface, navigate to the page you'd like to work with and double-click it to open in edit mode. Select the Comments component and double-click to edit.

2 In the Date Format tab, specify the date format to display the comments' publish date.

Comment Date Format

Comment components will display in the new date format.

Comment component display

How to add a Rating component

1   From the Websites interface, navigate to the page you'd like to add the ratings component. Double-click to open it in edit mode.

2   From the Sidekick, on the Components tab, select Social Collaboration. Drag and drop the Rating component into to the paragraph system.

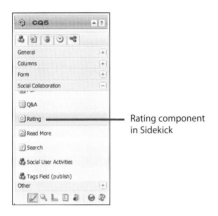 Rating component
in Sidekick

3   Configure the Text and Labels as shown.

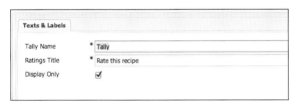

Text and Labels configuration

4   Confirm that the component has been successfully added by logging in as a user, going to the page, and adding a rating.

The rating component will display the total users rated and the average rating.

Rating component display

How to add the Forum component

The Forum component lets you display a list of forum topics where users can comment. It is different than the Comments component in that it structures comments into conversations.

1   Navigate to the page to which you'd like to add the forum and open it in edit mode.

2   From the Sidekick, select Social Collaboration and then drag and drop the Forum component into the paragraph system.

   The system prompts you to add the details.

3   Add a topic for the forum and a brief description.

4   Configure the Forum settings.

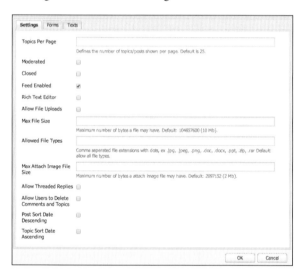

Configure Forum settings

TIP ▶ Often you will want to put a size limit on images and files; big files can be expensive for your infrastructure and create a poor user experience if other users have to wait a long time to download them.

5 Configure the topic and comments from the Forms tab.

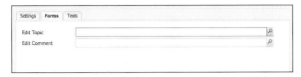

Configure Forms tab

6 Configure the display text in the Texts tab.

Configure display text: It is generally a best practice to include consistent messages for user-generated content. For example, "Be the first to create a topic…"

Once it has been added to the page, the forum component will display the forum title and comment count for the specific topic.

Forum component display

How to create a blog page

1 Open the Websites interface and select the website for the new blog page. Click New on the toolbar and choose New Page from the drop-down menu.

2 In the Create Page dialog box, enter the title and name of the page and select the Blog template. Click Create.

Create Page dialog box

3 To add a new blog entry, open the new page and click Add Entry. Add a blog post title and content with a rich text editor.

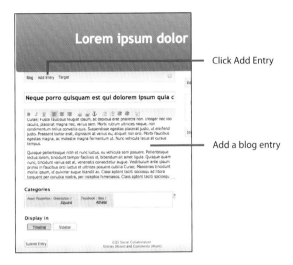

Click Add Entry

Add a blog entry

The blog post will be displayed with the commenting option enabled.

Blog display, with commenting

Community console management features

The Community console has enhanced views, with list and card view. Console features support most of the required actions needed by the administrator/moderator.

View options

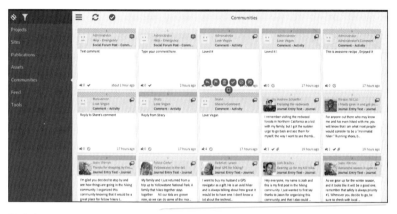

Card view

List view

View options: Navigation and Filter

Navigation icon

Navigation menu

Filter icon

Filter view: Lets the moderator filter
by content type, moderation status,
features, timeline, and sentiments

MODERATION CONTROL PANEL

A. Lets user reply

B. Flag the comment/reply

C. Delete from the system

D. Approve the comment/reply/forum/blog post (differentiate the objects with icons)

E. Deny/reject the comment/reply/forum/blog post

F. Mark the object as spam

G. View the content within the context of the page

Moderation control

By clicking the user name, the moderator gets to see the activity and segments for the selected user.

User's activity stream

≡ ‹   User Detail

USER DETAILS

Authorizable Id   **admin**

Email

About Me

Birthday

Family Name   **Administrator**

Given Name

Gender

Administrator

ACTIVITY STREAM

Address

🖻 - 20 hours ago - Administrator - Neque porro quisquam est qui dol...

City

State/Region

Vestibulum sagittis nulla feugiat, malesuada nisi sed, mattis velit. Aliquam erat volutpat. Integer mi tellus, euismod eu mi vitae, iaculis aliquet urna. Sed sagittis rutrum risus a suscipit. Mauris non porta diam. Vivamus sit amet varius nisi.

Postal Code

ENGAGEMENT

🖻 - 2 days ago - Administrator - Community

Scoring

communityScore - 300

Test comment

Badges

No badges

🖻 - 2 days ago - Administrator - Community

SEGMENTS

Type your comment here.

Insights

No insight segments

User detail view

How to create a Facebook cloud service configuration

1 Click Tools from the AEM home page.

2 On the Tools page, in the navigation pane on the left, expand Tools > Cloud Services.

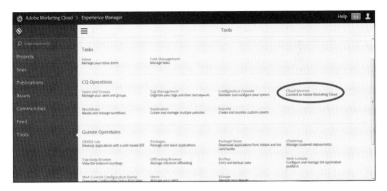

Cloud Services link on AEM home page (Mobile UI)

3 Double-click Facebook Connect to open it in a new browser tab. Click the plus icon to the right of Available Configurations.

4 In the Create Configuration dialog box, enter the Title and then click Create.

5 In the Facebook Connect Configuration dialog box, open the Settings tab. Enter the App ID/API Key for the Facebook application. (You can find this information at https://developers.facebook.com/apps.)

6 Enter the App Secret for the Facebook application and click Add User Group. Choose the desired group from the drop-down list. Select Create Users and deselect Mask User IDs.

7 Switch to the User Permissions tab. Select the Facebook permissions you would like to request from end users.

8 Click OK to save the new configuration.

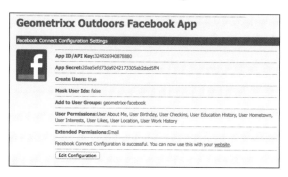

Facebook cloud service configuration

How to create a Twitter cloud service configuration

1 From the AEM home page, click Tools.

2 Click Cloud Services and double-click Twitter Connect to open it in a new browser tab. Expand the Available Configurations tree.

3 In the Create Configuration dialog box, enter a Title and click Create.

4 Enter the App ID/API Key for the Twitter application. (You can find this information at https://dev.twitter.com/apps.)

5 Enter the App Secret for the Twitter application and click Add User Group.

6 Choose the desired group from the drop-down list. Select Create Users and deselect Mask User IDs.

7 Click OK to save the new configuration.

Twitter cloud service configuration

Apply cloud service configurations to your website

1 From the AEM home page, click Websites. Navigate to the site you want to add cloud service configurations to.

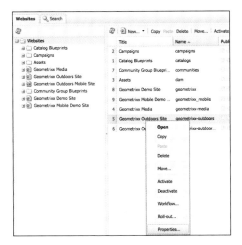

Web page cloud service configuration

2 Select Properties and open the Cloud Services tab. Click Add Service.

3 Select Facebook Connect and then click OK.

4 From the drop-down list, choose fbconnect (or whatever name you specified earlier for your Facebook connection).

5 Follow the same steps to add a Twitter Connect.

6 Click OK.

Web page cloud service configuration

How to test social login

1 From the AEM home page, click Websites. Navigate to the page where you've added the social login component.

2 Double-click the component to open the login dialog box and select Sign In With Twitter or Sign In With Facebook. To test that everything works, go to preview mode so you can test it out.

3 If you are not already logged in to the application, enter your login credentials in the fields provided. You may need to grant permission to Facebook to access your profile data.

4 Once you're logged in, the toolbar at the top of the page will show that you're signed in.

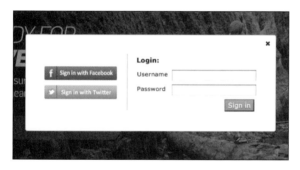

Test social login

11

Segmentation and Campaigns

The technology of AEM can sometimes be quite abstract. This chapter speaks to your inner marketer by discussing segmentations and campaigns. You'll soon discover just how AEM's tools help you accomplish all those big ideas.

Campaigns are generally used to draw visitors into a relationship or encourage them to make a purchase. AEM's segmentation and campaign management opens the door to agile marketing strategies that appeal to users on a personal level.

Segmentation

In marketing, it is all about getting the right content to the right person at the right time. To do this with AEM, you'll first need to define your target audiences, such as women who like winter sports. Then you'll create rules, which are called segments, to identify when someone belongs to this group. For example, gender=female and sport=skiing or snowboarding. Segments then allow you to personalize the user experience to these targeted groups, as you can promote women's ski gear or provide discounts on ski gear for first-time shoppers through the use of teasers.

How to create a segment

Segments are the rules that allow you to determine when someone meets a specific condition, in which you can target applicable messages to them. The hope is if you deliver personalized and relevant content that anticipates visitors' needs, they will be more likely to give your website repeat business.

1   From the AEM welcome screen, click Tools. Alternatively, you can click the Tools button in the AEM toolbar. Select the Segmentation folder on the left.

2   Click New on the toolbar to create a new segment.

Segmentation folder containing a list of segments available for use on a campaign

New button to create a new segment

Tools button

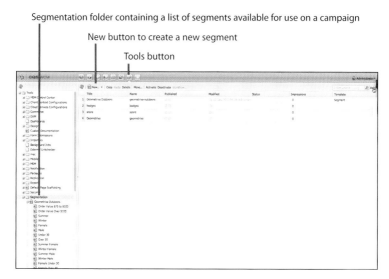

Creating a new segment

3 Create a name for the segment and select the Segment template type from the list. Click Create.

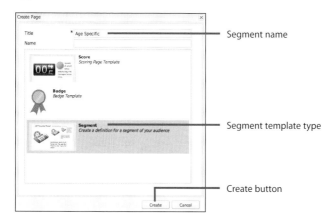

Segment name

Segment template type

Create button

Name the segment

4   Right-click the newly created segment and choose Open from the context menu.

Right-click the segment name and choose Open.

5   In the segment editor, right-click the component and choose New from the context menu to set a segment rule.

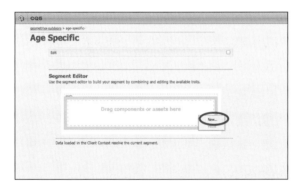

Right-click the segment component to add details.

6 Under Segmentation, select a component and click OK to drop the component.

The User Age component is used in this example.

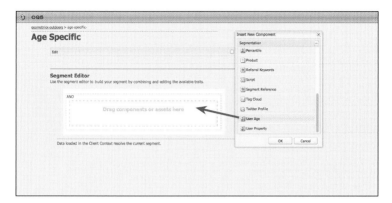

Segmentation component

7 In the segment editor, right-click the component and choose Edit from the context menu.

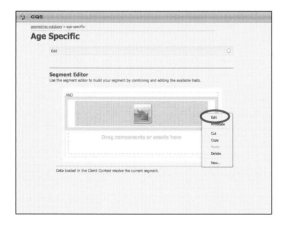

Edit function in the component context menu

TIP ▶ You can also double-click the component to edit it.

8 Set an operator and an associated value from the drop-down for the component.

In this example, the operator is set as equal to or older than 50.

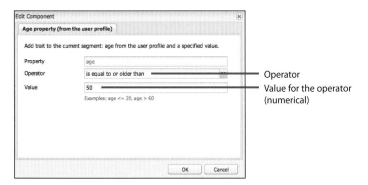

Component details

9 Once a segment operator and value has been set, you can test the segment by clicking the Client Context button on the Sidekick.

System warning that segment is not valid for the profile information loaded in Client Context

Client Context button

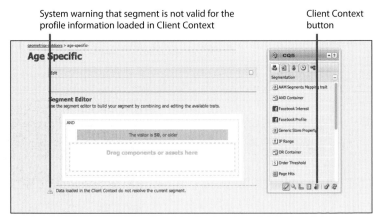

System warning about the segment

10 In the Client Context, click the Age tag and edit the age.

Age property in the Client Context

11 Set the age to 51 to match the operator and value condition. Notice that the segment component turns green, and the warning notification is now resolved confirming that the segment is tested successfully.

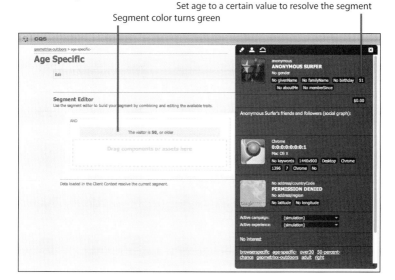

Segment turns green when conflict is resolved

Campaigns, leads, and email newsletters

Now that you've created your segments, you can harness the power of AEM's campaign, leads, and email newsletter tools.

Dashboard view

1 Access the Campaigns Dashboard by clicking the Campaigns button, either on the AEM welcome screen or from the AEM toolbar.

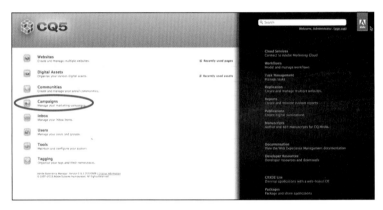

Campaigns link

Campaigns button on the AEM toolbar

AEM displays a Dashboard view of all campaigns, lists, segments, and reports.

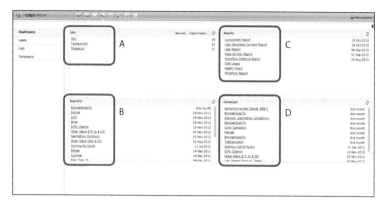

Campaigns Dashboard

A. Lists: Create a distribution list of people to send newsletters.

B. Segments: A view of all the available segments in AEM; this is also where you can edit the segment component.

C. Reports: Provides a snapshot of various activities such as page activity and user-generated content that can be configured for hourly or daily snapshots.

D. Campaigns: A concise view of all the currently active campaigns and on what pages

How to create a new lead

1 Navigate to the Campaigns Dashboard (AEM home page > Campaigns). Select the Leads option in the left pane and click New in the toolbar.

Leads menu item   New button to create a new lead

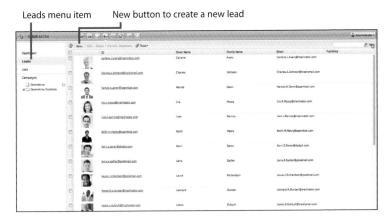

Campaigns Dashboard

2 In the Create Lead dialog box, set the relevant properties for the lead such as email, name, gender, date of birth, and so on. Click Save to create a new lead.

Create a new lead

How to create a new list

1 Navigate to the Campaigns Dashboard (AEM Home > Campaigns). Select the Lists option in the left pane and click New.

Lists menu item   New button to create a new list

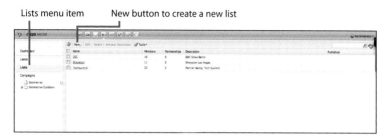

Campaigns Dashboard

2 Enter a name for the list and an optional ID. Enter any extra details in the About field. Click Save to save the list.

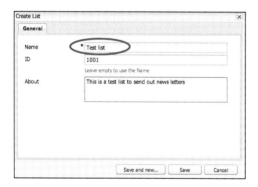

Create a list name and add any relevant details.

How to add a lead to a list

1 Navigate to the Campaigns Dashboard (AEM Home > Campaigns). Right-click the list you want to add leads to and choose Tools > Import Leads from the context menu.

Tools option in the lead's context menu   Import leads option in the Tools submenu

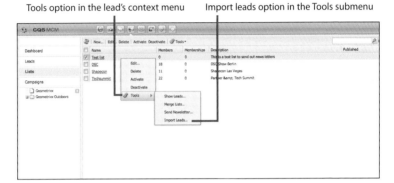

Right-click the list to access the Tools submenu

2 Enter the leads' data in comma-separated values format in the open text field to set leads for a list. Click Next.

Import leads

NOTE ▶ The first row will always be the table header.

AEM displays the lead(s) in tabular format.

3 Click Next to import the lead(s) into this list.

Preview leads to import

4 Enter a name for the list and click Import.

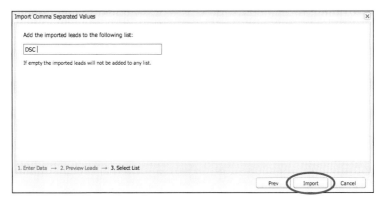

Select list and click Import.

How to send newsletters via email to a list

1 Navigate to the Campaigns Dashboard. (AEM Home > Campaigns). Select the Lists option on the left.

2 To initiate the email chain, right-click a list you want to send newsletters to and choose Tools > Send Newsletter from the context menu.

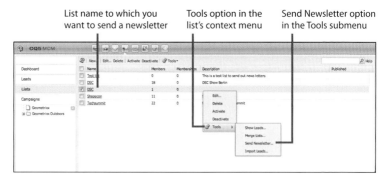

Send a newsletter

3 In the Send Newsletter dialog box, click the search icon (magnifying glass) to select a particular newsletter. Click OK.

4 Click Next.

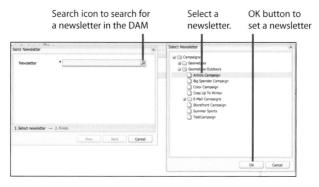

Send newsletter feature

5   Click Send to send the selected newsletter to the associated leads
    on that list.

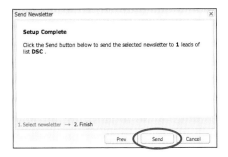

Send newsletter

How to create a new campaign with a teaser

1   Navigate to the Campaigns Dashboard. (AEM Home > Cam-
    paigns). Select the Campaigns section on the left pane and click
    New to create a new campaign.

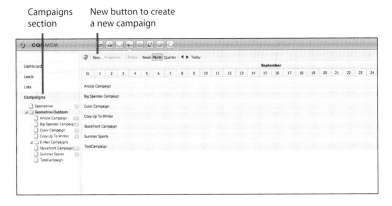

Create a new campaign

2 Enter a name for the new campaign and select the Campaign template. Click Create to create the campaign.

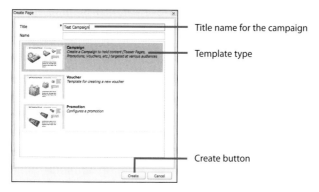

Title name for the campaign

Template type

Create button

Campaign name

3 Navigate to the new campaign in the list and click New in the toolbar.

4 In the Create Experience dialog box, name the experience and select Teaser Page as the experience type from the available templates. Click Create.

New campaign name in the Campaigns section

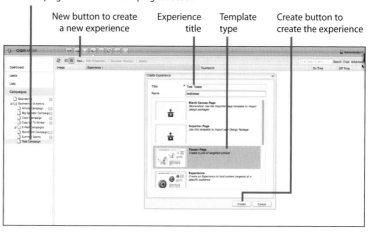

New button to create a new experience

Experience title

Template type

Create button to create the experience

Creating a new teaser

5 Right-click the new teaser and choose Properties from the context menu. Or, click the Properties button on the toolbar.

6 In the Properties dialog box, set relevant metadata tags for the
teaser. Click the Location field's search icon to set the teaser for
a particular page.

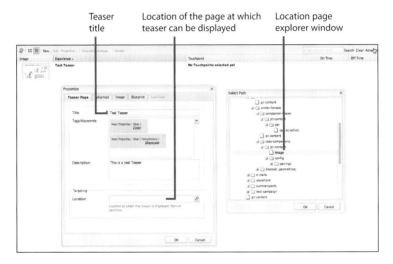

Teaser properties

You can also associate a teaser with a particular segment to
apply segment-specific rules so that the teaser is displayed only
when certain conditions are met from a client perspective at a
particular page.

7 Click the Advanced tab and click Add Item to add a segment to the teaser.

Advanced tab — Segments section (click the small arrow to expand it) — Add Item link to add a segment

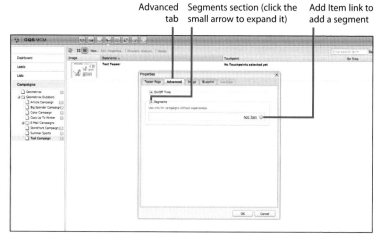

Adding a segment to the teaser

8 Select from the list of available segments and click OK to finish associating a segment to the teaser.

Search icon to search for a segment — Explorer window that displays the available segments in AEM

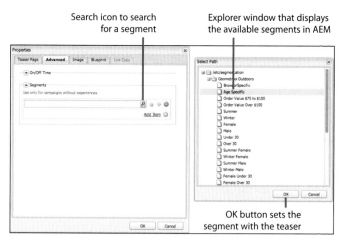

OK button sets the segment with the teaser

Adding a segment to a teaser

9 To assign relevant content on the teaser, select the teaser and click the Edit button on the toolbar (or right-click the teaser and choose Edit from the context menu).

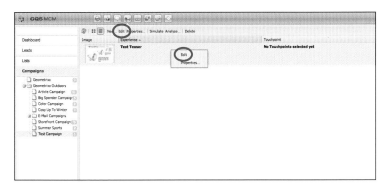

Two ways to get to the Edit option

10 In the teaser editor, right-click the Content component and choose New from the context menu.

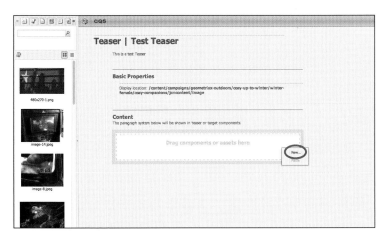

Add new component to the teaser

This example uses an image component dragged from the Sidekick.

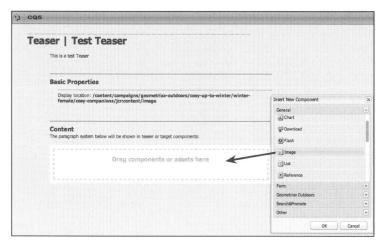

Image component in the sidekick

11 To add an image, right-click the newly added image component and choose Edit from the context menu.

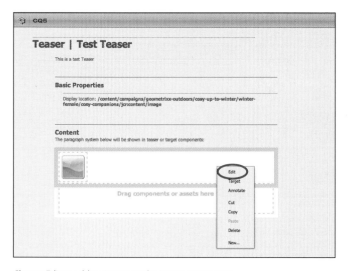

Choose Edit to add an image on the image component.

12 Select an image from the content explorer or click the content area to upload an image from the DAM.

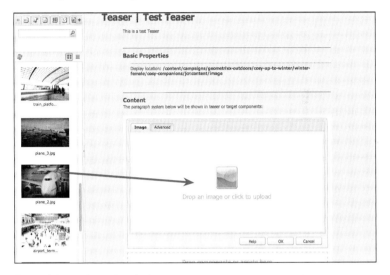

Drag and drop an image into the image component

Multivariate components

A multivariate component allows you to see the click-through rate (CTR) for a particular component on a page. Upon receiving a page request from a client, the multivariate component assigned to that page triggers for display and collects the data to analyze the click-through rate. This feature allows you to see which features or images are effective at garnering traffic and interest on your website.

How to add a multivariate component

1   Navigate to a page where you want to add a multivariate compo-
    nent. Drag the Multivariate Testing component from the Sidekick
    and drop it on an available paragraph system on the page.

    NOTE ▶ If the Multivariate Testing component is not appearing in
    the Sidekick, enter the design mode of the page and click Edit on the
    Design Of Par component. Then select the Multivariate component
    from the General category and click OK.

Drag and drop the Multivariate Testing component on the page

2   To add content, click the Edit button on the component.

Edit button to add content

3 Click the Banners tab and drop in an image to associate the banner with the multivariate component. You can add more banners by clicking the Add button.

Banner tab

Add button to add more
banners for tracking purposes

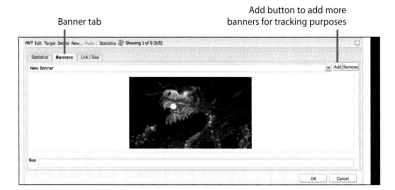

Associate an image to the multivariate component.

4 After adding all the banners, click the Statistics button to display the total impressions for each banner and their click-through rates.

NOTE ▸ To clear the statistics, click Reset Statistics button in the Statistics tab

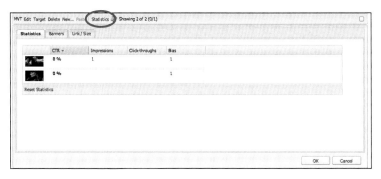

Statistics button

ExactTarget integration

ExactTarget—a powerful add-on to the AEM framework—lets you manage and send email created in AEM. By integrating AEM with ExactTarget, you can do the following:

- Create emails in AEM and publish them to ExactTarget for distribution.
- Set action of an AEM form to create an ExactTarget subscriber.

Exact Target can be configured with AEM by selecting it from the Adobe Marketing Cloud from the home page or by directly accessing http://<*hostname*>:<*port*>/etc/cloudservices.html.

NOTE ▶ The user must have an account with ExactTarget to enable it in AEM and utilize any API to send out direct marketing emails.

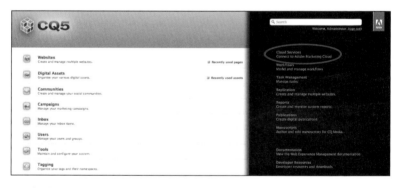

Cloud services link on the welcome screen of AEM

1   Click ExactTarget and then click Configure Now.

ExactTarget information   Configure Now
bar to connect with AEM   button

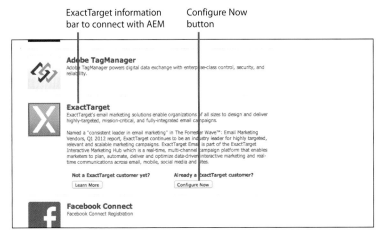

AEM home page > Cloud Services page

2   Enter a configuration name and select the ExactTarget template
from the list.

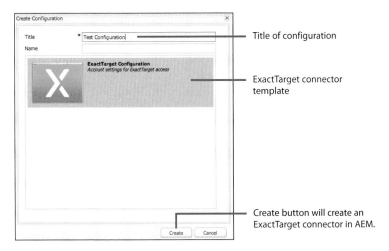

Create Configuration dialog box

After creating the ExactTarget Connector component, AEM opens the configuration window to edit the login credentials and API to connect to from ExactTarget.

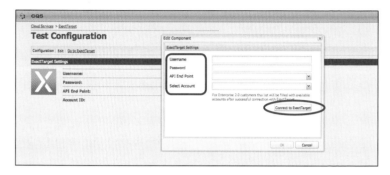

12

Administration Basics

The administrative features available in Adobe Experience Manager could fill an entire book. Since most of them are primarily for highly experienced administrators or developers (as opposed to general business users), this book does not cover the majority of them. The features described in this chapter apply to business users who also act as administrators for their teams. While you may not be the person using these tools, understand that they are available to help your team manage various websites.

Users and groups

Like any enterprise application, AEM allows for the management of users and groups, including provisioning their roles and permissions.

How to create a user

1 From the AEM home page, click Users to access the Users interface. You can also access it via the Users icon on the AEM toolbar.

   TIP ▶ Consider changing the password for the admin user and limiting its use to a single person. You can create more administrative users, but "admin" should remain a special account.

Users icon on the AEM toolbar

2 To create a new user, click the Edit button and choose Create > Create User from the drop-down menu.

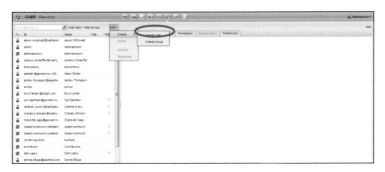

Edit > Create > Create User

3 Fill out the Create User form and click Create.

Create New User

The new user is created and appears under the user and group list on the left.

4 Double-click the new user to confirm that the details are correct.

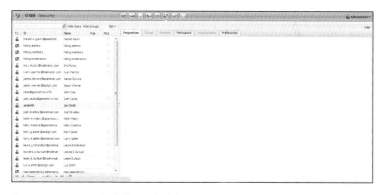

The new user appears in the list on the left.

How to create a group

1 From the AEM home page, click Users to access the Users interface. You can also access it via the Users icon on the AEM toolbar.

Users icon on the AEM toolbar

2 To create a new group, click the Edit button and choose Create > Create Group from the drop-down menu.

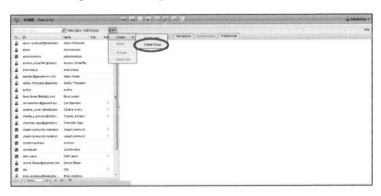

Edit > Create > Create Group

3 Fill out the Create Group form and click Create.

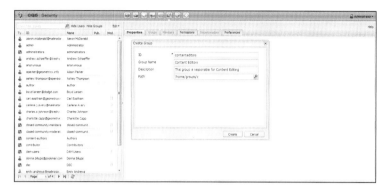

New group details

The new group is created and appears under the user and group list on the left side of the Users interface.

New group as it appears in the list

You can select one or more users and add them to a specific group.

4   Select the group on the left side pane and click the Members tab. Now you can search for specific users and drag and drop them, which will make the users part of the group.

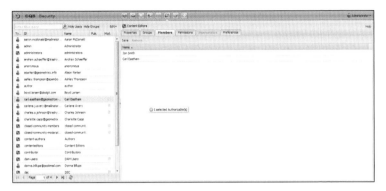

Select one or more users to add to the newly created group.

NOTE ▶ Group permissions will take precedence over individual user permissions in the case of a conflict.

How to edit permissions for users and groups

1   From the Users interface, navigate to the user or group whose permissions you'd like to edit. Click the Permissions tab.

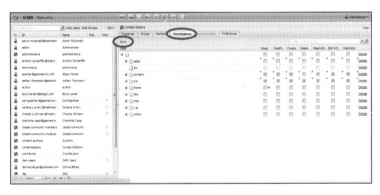

Permissions tab and details

2   Assign permissions by clicking the check boxes.

3   Click Save to save the permission settings for the user or group.

How to impersonate an author

Often you need to duplicate the role of an author with exact permissions and group settings as that of an original author. In order to achieve that easily, AEM provides a way to impersonate an author.

TIP ▶ If you don't see this option, you don't have permissions to impersonate users.

1 Navigate to the Users interface and select the user you want to impersonate.

2 Click the Impersonators tab.

3 From the user list on the left side, select the other user who needs to impersonate the author.

4 Drag and drop that user onto the impersonator area of the original author and click Save.

Drag and drop the user into the impersonator area and then click Save.

Impersonating a user

NOTE ▶ You can also impersonate users if you click your name in the top right corner. In the Impersonate field, you can type the person's name or select the user you want to impersonate.

Reports, packages, and external link checkers

These tools allow you to manage migration content between environments, gain valuable insights about your websites, and find broken links on your website.

How to create reports

1 From the AEM home page, go to the Tools section and click Reports under the Operations header.

Tools interface in the touch UI

TIP ▶ In production, you'll be using the Classic UI you've seen elsewhere in the book. In the Classic UI, click the Tools icon in the top navigation, and then navigate to the Reports section.

The out-of-the-box AEM reports are displayed.

The Tools > Reports link opens a list of AEM reports.

2   Double-click any specific report from the list to view data.

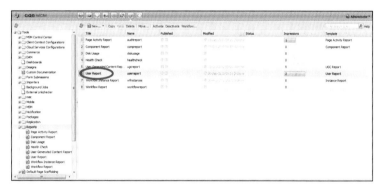

Double-click the report to view data.

How to work with packages

Packages enable the importing and exporting of repository content. For example, you can use packages to install new functionality, transfer content between instances, and back up repository content.

> **TIP** ▶ Package Manager is quite powerful. It can blow up your AEM instance, but it's also one of the most useful tools at your disposal. If you limit your Package Manager access to system administrators or capable, responsible employees and follow the best practices defined by Adobe in the AEM documentation, you'll be grateful for this interface.

1   In order to access packages, click Tools from the AEM home page and then click Packages under Granite Operations.

Tools > Packages (in the touch UI)

> **TIP** ▶ In the classic UI version, you'll see package manager on the default welcome screen when you log in, called Packages. You can also click the home icon (stacked cubes) in the top left corner, which will take you to the welcome screen.

2   Click the Adobe group on the left pane, which shows all the out-of-the-box packages available in AEM.

Packages available out-of-the-box in AEM

How to use an external link checker

You will only be able to access this screen if you have the correct permissions. The Web Console or Felix Console is primarily used by administrators or developers to set variables for AEM.

1   Log in to Felix Console here: http://<<host>>:<<port>>/felix/console or select Web Console in the lower right corner on the AEM welcome page.

2   Enter the administrator user credentials.

3 Choose Main > Components.

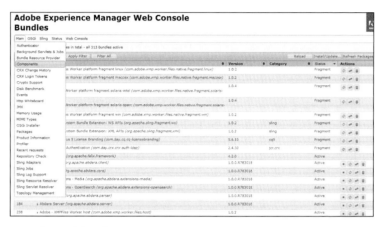

AEM web console bundles

4 Search for DAY CQ Link Checker Services. Four of them are available.

Configuration service available for link checker

5   Click Day CQ Link Externalizer for configuring the server-specific domain URLs.

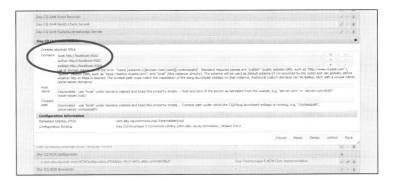

Configuration service for domain-specific configuration

6   After configuring the URLs, click Save.

7   In order to enable or disable the rewrite of URLs or link checking, click the Day CQ Link Checker Transformer Service Settings link.

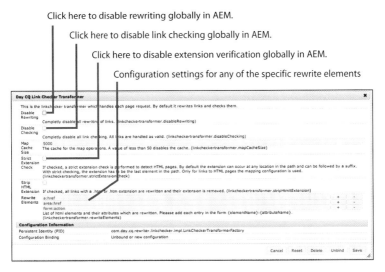

Day CQ Link Checker Transformer

How to verify that links are valid

An external link checker is provided within AEM. The link checker scans all content pages, generates a list of all valid and invalid links, and marks invalid links as broken on the individual content pages.

1 Click Tools from the AEM home page and select External Linkchecker.

External Linkchecker

2 Double-click the External Linkchecker to open a detailed view in a new window.

Detailed view of External Linkchecker

The link checker view provides detailed information for each and every link available in AEM. It includes:

- Status of the link
- URL
- Time since the link was last validated
- Time since the link was last available
- Time since the link was last accessed

Index